"In a political era where we are bombarded daily with reports of racism and discrimination, it is easy to feel helpless and withdraw. Anneliese Singh's workbook is a practical guide to actively engaging and participating in social justice on a personal and societal level. Singh draws on best practices, research, and advocacy to create pathways to restore hope in humanity and to create the self-efficacy needed to be a change agent. What a gift!"

—**Edward Delgado-Romero, PhD**, associate dean for faculty and staff services, professor and licensed psychologist, College of Education, University of Georgia

"Racism is America's original sin. It is woven into the fabric of this country, and is an inextricable part of this nation's history. Racism is psychologically and spiritually damaging, yet the sad reality is that in the current political climate racism has been emboldened. Anneliese Singh has given us a desperately needed gift in this racial healing workbook. For those who are social justice activists, or just people who want to understand themselves as racial beings, Singh's workbook is a psychological guide and spiritual salve for facilitating our own racial healing. It is destined to become a classic!"

—**Kevin Cokley, PhD**, Oscar and Annie Mauzy Regents Professor for educational research and development, professor in the department of educational psychology and African and African diaspora studies, and author of the book *The Myth of Black Anti-Intellectualism*

"This is the book you've been waiting for, even if you didn't know you were waiting for it! Anneliese Singh makes a racial healing path accessible, practical, and comprehensive for anyone willing to pursue it. This handbook is personal, straightforward, honest, and inviting, and honors the system of racism in all its complexity. It is the rare kind of book I can recommend to my family, my friends, my colleagues, my clients, and to myself. An important contribution to our individual and collective paths toward liberation!"

—**Jen Willsea, MTS**, Atlanta-based social justice and anti-racism facilitator, consultant, and coach

"Race and healing? Not words you often see together! Yet Anneliese Singh has brought her gifts together as a healer, a scholar, a clinician, and an activist to weave a heartfelt and liberating book of hope. Whether you're White, a person of color, or multiracial, Singh invites us all—through personal stories, reflection exercises, self-assessments, and an impressive integration of history and the social sciences—to engage in the lifelong practice of racial transformation for ourselves and our communities. This is a gift and a balm for the racial wounds we all carry!"

> —**Alvin N. Alvarez, PhD**, professor in the department of counseling and dean of the
> college of health and social sciences at San Francisco State University, and coeditor of
> *The Cost of Racism for People of Color*

"Anneliese Singh's *The Racial Healing Handbook* is a must-have resource for all educators and mental health workers, and for anyone interested in creating a more racially just world. Singh masterfully weaves together theory, empirical research, and narrative to inform her discussion of the key elements for racial healing for people of color and White individuals. Singh's strength is her ability to translate research into developmentally appropriate, practical activities that will stimulate deep reflection and action. As such, she offers a nice balance of cognitive, emotional, and behavioral exploration. I can't wait to use the handbook and practical exercises in my classes and my work with community members."

> —**Helen A. Neville, PhD**, professor in the department of educational psychology and
> African American studies at the University of Illinois at Urbana-Champaign; past
> president of the Society for the Psychological Study of Culture, Ethnicity, and Race; and
> coeditor of *The Myth of Racial Color Blindness* and *The Cost of Racism for People of Color*

The Social Justice Handbook Series

As culture evolves, we need new tools to help us cope and interact with our social world in ways that feel authentic and empowered. That's why New Harbinger created the *Social Justice Handbook* series—a series that teaches readers how to use practical, psychology-based tools to challenge and transform dominant culture, both in their daily lives and in their communities.

Written by thought leaders in the fields of psychology, sociology, gender, and ethnic studies, the *Social Justice Handbook* series offers evidence-based strategies for coping with a broad range of social inequities that impact quality of life. As research has shown us, social oppression can lead to mental health issues such as depression, anxiety, trauma, lowered self-esteem, and self-harm. These handbooks provide accessible social analysis, as well as thoughtful activities and exercises based on the latest psychological methods to help readers unlearn internalized negative messages, resist social inequities, transform their communities, and challenge dominant culture to be equitable for all.

The handbooks also serve as a hands-on resource for therapists who wish to integrate an understanding and acknowledgement of how multiple social issues impact their clients to provide relevant and supportive care.

For a complete list of books in
the *Social Justice Handbook* series,
visit newharbinger.com.

THE
RACIAL
HEALING
HANDBOOK

PRACTICAL ACTIVITIES TO HELP YOU
CHALLENGE PRIVILEGE, CONFRONT SYSTEMIC RACISM
& ENGAGE IN COLLECTIVE HEALING

ANNELIESE A. SINGH, PhD, LPC

New Harbinger Publications, Inc.

Visit http://www.newharbinger.com/42709 for a downloadable *clinician's guide* and a downloadable *reading group guide* for this book.

Publisher's Note

This publication is designed to provide accurate and authoritative information in regard to the subject matter covered. It is sold with the understanding that the publisher is not engaged in rendering psychological, financial, legal, or other professional services. If expert assistance or counseling is needed, the services of a competent professional should be sought.

In consideration of evolving American English usage standards, and reflecting a commitment to equity for all genders, "they/them" is used in this book to denote singular persons.

NEW HARBINGER PUBLICATIONS is a registered trademark of New Harbinger Publications, Inc.

Distributed in Canada by Raincoast Books

The figure "Racial Identity Development" in chapter 1 is adapted from the work of Marla Rowe Gorosh and Kathy McGrail and John and Joy Hoffman. Reproduced by permission of Marla Rowe Gorosh and Kathy McGrail.

"Examples of Racial Microaggressions" in chapter 6 is reproduced from "Table 1: Examples of Racial Microaggressions" (pp. 282–283) in Sue, D. W., Capodilupo, C. M., Torino, G. C., Bucceri, J. M., Holder, A. M. B., Nadal, K. L., and Esquilin, M. (2007). "Racial microaggressions in everyday life: Implications for clinical practice." *American Psychologist*, 62(4), 271–286.

Cover design by Sara Christian; Interior design by Michele Waters-Kermes;
Acquired by Ryan Buresh; Edited by Rona Bernstein

All Rights Reserved

Library of Congress Cataloging-in-Publication Data on file

Printed in the United States of America

25 24 23

15 14 13 12 11 10 9

For my beloved, Lauren Lukkarila,
who supports me in every step of my own racial healing journey.

For Jasbir Singh, Diane Singh, and Ravi Singh—your courage is with me always.

For Priyanka Sinha—you are my dearest friend, mirror, and anchor on this racial healing journey.

To New Orleans and to India—you both taught me not only the brutal realities of racism, but also the pathways toward racial justice and healing.

To my fellow Sikhs—may we cultivate *chardi kala* and *sarbhat da bhala* in building a more racially just world.

Contents

Foreword

Confession time: I was late—very, very late—turning in this foreword. As in, a few hours before the passing of the absolute final, final deadline late.

And although I wouldn't normally think my tardiness necessary to mention at the outset of someone else's book, in this instance, the reason for it is entirely related to the subject matter of this important volume.

To be specific, for most of December 2018, my family and I were the recipients of an onslaught of hateful phone calls, texts, and tweets from white supremacists who managed to find and release our cell phone numbers and address to the general public and to threaten harm not just to myself but also to my wife and two daughters. Long story short, after much effort, we have weathered the storm, turned over the harassers' information to the proper authorities, and taken the necessary measures to protect ourselves from future threats.

But the bigger question is about how we, as a society and a culture more broadly, can protect ourselves from the poison of white supremacy. Not just in its most blatant iterations, as with the kinds of twisted souls who have spent the better part of a month harassing my family, but even when it comes in a smoother, less obvious package, as it so often does. Or when it carries the power and authority of the state, as with disproportionate police violence or immigration enforcement against persons of color.

Because for every white man like myself who has the resources (and frankly the power) to go after the racists who terrorize me and mine, there are literally millions of people of color—especially women of color, and LGBTQ folks of color, and poor folks of color—who do not. Who carry around the same fears, indeed greater ones than I, but for whom society extends not one-tenth as much sympathy or the kind of response it does for me.

Not that society *shouldn't* respond to hateful racist and anti-Semitic threats like those directed at my family, of course. It should. But until such a response is the norm—and until people of color can feel safe going to law enforcement to protect *them* from white supremacists, rather than worrying that law enforcement is but another instrument of white supremacy—this culture will have a lot of work to do. Obviously at present, we are a long way from that time.

That's where this wonderful and vital volume comes in. I have known Anneliese Singh for a little more than thirty years now. Our history is extensive: from anti-apartheid work at Tulane University in the 1980s to fighting for reproductive justice in Louisiana and challenging the political candidacies of neo-Nazi David Duke in the early 1990s, we have been through a lot together. I am ecstatic to call her a friend, a colleague, and a teacher.

In this workbook, Dr. Singh teaches us all, myself very much included, how to truly identify racism, both internalized and systemic, and to take action for justice and equity. And not from a position of guilt or shame, but from one of strength and commitment. Importantly, she shows us the connections between the tortured national history of racism and white supremacy and the issues we face today, illustrating how we have for so long carried the scars of that injury with us and transmitted them like a virus down through the generations. And she reminds us of the harm racism does to all: to people of color as its targets, to be sure; and also to white folks, who wind up as the collateral damage of a system created for our benefit, but which, in the long run, injures us all.

Weaving personal, historical, and analytical narratives with dexterity, humility, and compassion, Anneliese shows us a path forward—at a vital moment in the history of the United States and the world. With xenophobic nationalism on the rise throughout the so-called white world (in the U.S. and Europe in particular), and with Trumpism taking longstanding racist tropes and weaponizing them in ways even more blatant than with previous American presidents, there could be no better time for a workbook of this nature.

Although the kinds of racism and anti-immigrant hysteria currently being whipped up around the world are hardly new, with modern technology spreading hate faster than ever and with the global economy leaving hundreds of millions of people behind, the atmosphere for reactionary and even neofascist politics, which seek to blame despised "others" for the problems of unemployment, crime, and other social ills, becomes even more toxic. While many authors and thinkers have weighed in so as to diagnose the problem, fewer have offered up personal and systemic measures one can take in the cause of freedom.

That's why I am so grateful for what Anneliese Singh has provided us in this volume. More than just an exploration of our national and global dilemma when it comes to racism and white supremacy, what *The Racial Healing Handbook* offers us is a blueprint, with practical steps all of us can utilize and deploy to get free from the personal and institutional barriers to racial equity and justice for all.

Like Anneliese, this book is resolute and bold, pulls no punches, and fundamentally tells the truth. Both she and the work she has produced here are indispensable to the struggle. It is an honor to know her and to heartily recommend her genius, on full display in *The Racial Healing Handbook*.

—Tim Wise
Antiracist educator, commentator, and author of
White Like Me: Reflections from a Privileged Son
Nashville, TN

Introduction

There are several basic premises of this workbook, the first of which is that our world is steeped in racism. Racism is a system of oppression that relies on beliefs that one race or group of people is superior to another based on biological characteristics, like skin color, facial features, and hair. White supremacy, the key driver of racism, designates White people as superior to people of color—which is just not true. There is no one race that is better than another.

In the system of racism, White and light-skinned folks are granted unearned privileges or advantages by society just because of their race. For instance, White folks get to see their societal value reflected back to them continuously—from seeing their histories in school textbooks and positive media portrayals to having the advantages of safe neighborhoods, quality education, high-paying jobs, access to good medical care, and greater health and well-being. Meanwhile, people of color experience a world that does not value them in the same way as it values White people, and they experience a lack of access to neighborhoods, schools, communities, and jobs, which in turn influences the quality of their overall health and well-being. Privileging one group of human beings over another in this way is obviously not fair.

A second premise of this workbook is that because we all grow up in a society steeped in racism, everyone learns explicit and implicit stereotyped messages in families, schools, and communities about who people of color and White people are. We end up learning these racialized stereotypes and acting on them consciously and unconsciously without much opportunity to unpack or critique them. In this manner, racism has created—and continues to create—wounds of pain, grief, and loss for *everyone* in society, both those devalued by racism and those who are in the dominant, privileged group.

When you internalize and come to believe stereotyped ideas of who other people are and who you are, it becomes challenging to understand how extensively we all are influenced by the context of white supremacy (Wise 2011). People of color have their opportunities and lives limited by the barriers they face and the way their experiences and identities are marginalized. And White people find themselves participating in a system in which they gain advantages that, as individuals, they may not have earned. This can lead to feelings of unease and guilt as they see people of color who don't have those advantages or when they witness overt racism. But so much of racism, especially in the current moment, is systemic—embedded into the structures that surround us, including our schools, governments, legal system, social programs, and more. Consider the following examples. School systems continue to use textbooks that center the history of White people, and when it comes to high school completion, Black and Latinx students have lower rates than their White peers—likely due to racist school environments and differential access to educational supports and resources (Sablich 2016). People of color have little representation in the US federal government; at the time of this writing, the House of Representatives is 75% White (Wolf 2018), and the US Senate is 90% White (Brown 2017). Black and Latinx Americans make up 32% of the US population, yet they constitute 56% of people who are incarcerated (NAACP n.d.). Asian and Pacific Islander Americans who are US citizens are consistently asked where they were "born" (Tran and Lee 2015), implying that they somehow are perpetually "foreign" to the United States. Native American/First Nation/Indigenous people see their images used as mascots for sports teams, which is a denigration of their culture (Leavitt et al. 2015). These are just a few examples of the widespread racism in our society—privileging one group (White people) while disadvantaging another group (people of color).

So while racism does exist, as a society we don't tend to have regular conversations about it, aside from social media posts and occasional town hall meetings, which is partly why it is hard to figure out what racism is, when it is happening, and what to do about it. On the one hand, you may be able to identify racism when it is happening, like when a family member, friend, or colleague makes a racist comment or joke. On the other hand, you might not know how to respond or interrupt this person, leaving you with a range of feelings, such as guilt, anger, fear, and sadness. Or you may feel that you are the target of the racist joke or comment and feel too stunned and shocked to respond. Racism can be truly overwhelming in our interpersonal interactions.

But, as extensive and overwhelming as racism can be, there is a third premise of this workbook: that you can begin healing from racism through changing your individual actions and interpersonal interactions.

When I talk about "healing from racism," what do I mean? Healing means you begin to unlearn the stereotyped racial messages you internalized about your own race and the race of others. It means you as an individual learn to recognize the wounds that racism creates in you, whether you are White or a person of color and whether you are conscious of these nicks and tears to your psyche or not. Healing means you open your eyes to the costs of racism, which are pretty much everywhere, and work to stop participating, either knowingly or actively, in the system of racism and white supremacy that was designed to favor some people and not others. You learn to notice how your race drives the differential privileges and access to needed resources you might receive.

The good news is that healing from racism is a process of proactive individual actions and strategies you can practice throughout your lifetime. And the even better news is that as you begin to heal from racism, you can learn to give folks in your personal and professional circles the opportunity to heal from racism too.

So, as you read this workbook, you will learn a recipe of sorts for individual actions you can take right now to be an active part of dismantling racism, while doing some important healing in the process. These endeavors aren't simple processes that will happen overnight, but they are processes you can start now, so you can be part of a generation of folks who did something about racism together.

Getting educated is a key part of ending racism, so let's talk a little more about what racism is and why healing from racism is an integral part of dismantling it.

WHAT IS RACISM, EXACTLY?

To understand racism, you have to understand *race* and *ethnicity*. In this workbook, you will see me use the word "race" as shorthand to describe both race and ethnicity—but there is a difference between them. *Race* is often defined as a biological construct, such as a shared genetic classification. *Ethnicity* refers to a group that shares a common or distinct ancestry and cultural practices, generally according to a geographic region and often with psychological attachment (Phinney 1990).

To make it even more complicated, race and ethnicity are just social constructions—elements of a system developed by humans to categorize people who "appear" to share common features. These constructs can and often do overlap. And often these words—which are frequently used inaccurately and have been scientifically disproven—were designed for racist practices. A good example is the word "Caucasian," a common term to describe the race of White people. The term comes from Blumenbach's racial classification system, in which he purported that God created Caucasians in his own image as the ideal race (Moses 2017). Then, Blumenbach designated other races that he deemed inferior to describe everyone else (e.g., Mongolian, Malayan, and Negroid). Blumenbach's system was later used to justify the enslavement of Black people in the US (Moses 2017), so his social construction of race had lasting effects. But guess what? The term "Caucasian" is also entirely inaccurate. My very brown and very Indian dad was born near the Caucasus Mountains, and his skin color was the furthest thing you could imagine from being "White." So you can see how the word "Caucasian" is not a helpful or accurate word to describe White people.

Nonetheless, White supremacy is real, and the amount of melanin that you have in your skin signals something to the world about the societal norms that will be applied to your presumed race. For instance, there are societal norms—the vestiges of colonization and enslavement practices—that value light skin over dark skin. In other words, these societal norms promote messages that Whites are the "ideal" race, which then puts folks of color in the non-ideal box. These messages then trickle into our media, schools, families, and communities, where we pick up these implicit and explicit messages without realizing it. This is why Asian American/Pacific Islanders face perpetual questions about their "foreign-ness" and Black men are viewed as "threats" or "dangerous"—because their skin color is outside the White "norm" and deemed less than. And of course, this social construction of race is wholly unjust and unfair.

So it's important to (1) keep in mind that race is not helpful as a social construction and (2) recognize and understand that racism really exists based on perceptions of what your race or the race of others might be. Long story short, race can be a pretty inaccurate social construction to describe who you really are. But your perceived race and the race you perceive of others matters a lot in society because of White supremacy. And that is what racism ultimately is: the construction of "races" from particular biological characteristics people have, and the use of this construction to lift up certain groups in society into a dominant class and keep other groups in a lower, oppressed class.

The system of racism is such that all people in the societies in which racism exists are affected by it. This is also why this book is written for everyone—those who are disadvantaged under White supremacy *and* those who benefit from it. The reality is, we all suffer under White supremacy and racism. And we all have the power to heal that suffering, too.

HEALING FROM RACISM: A DARING PROPOSITION

Each chapter of this workbook will take you step by step through a given strategy of healing from racism. Each step will relate to you no matter what your racial identity is; this workbook is for people of color *and* White people to engage in racial healing strategies alongside one another. There may be ways you diverge in your exploration of healing from racism if you are a person of color or White, but along the way you get to take a peek into what another reader from a different social identity or subject position might be doing to foster their part of healing from the pain and wounds of racism. For instance, both people of color and White folks internalize racism that may be easy or challenging to recognize, yet there is a distinct difference in how this happens. If you are a person of color, you have internalized negative messages and beliefs about your race, and if you are White, you have internalized a sense of dominance related to your race.

Why did I want to address both White folks and folks of color together in the same workbook? Well, I myself grew up with a lot of the racial complexities we will talk about in this book. My mom was White and her family had immigrated to the land we now call the United States multiple generations ago. My dad was a Sikh, turban-wearing guy who emigrated from India in the 1950s. In retrospect, as their mixed-race child, I saw so many missed opportunities for my mom and dad to talk about how racism influenced their relationship. For instance, I never heard how my mom felt about the racism she saw my dad experience because of his dark skin, turban, and immigrant status. I also never got to hear how he felt when she was silent about the racism she saw him and our family experience. Because my parents were in the throes of experiencing racism as an interracial couple and didn't quite have the words to talk about what was happening to them, I also didn't know what I was experiencing when it came to the system of racism and the messages I was learning about what it meant to be White or a person of color.

So, after these experiences surrounding race in my family, I set about on a healing journey myself. I learned that healing from racism wasn't a one-time thing, a few workshops to attend, or even a counselor's office to frequent. I learned that healing from racism comprised several important healing strategies to keep engaging with over time. I pursued training in counseling and psychology, immersing myself in studies by leading multicultural scholars on race (including Derald Wing Sue, who wrote the afterword in this book), looking for more specifics on the harm that occurs from racism. I knew what racism felt like when I experienced it, because even when it was subtle I could feel it in my bones. I also reconnected with racial justice movements I had been involved in and fellow activists I had shared space with (including my friend Tim Wise, who also wrote the foreword to this book).

In doing all of this, I not only became more educated about the empirical studies and racial justice movements detailing what racism is, but I also dug deep into how racism personally impacted me in multiple areas of my life—and as a human being. And I adopted a "recovery mindset": I realized I might not be able to save the world from racism, but I was going to identify ways I had internalized racist ideas and stereotypes about the world. Part of this recovery included identifying ways I could act differently when I encountered racism in day-to-day life, so as to be genuinely antiracist, and perhaps inspire others to do the same. In the process, I found that adopting this intentional recovery framework where I was engaging individual strategies of healing—such as learning about my cultural background and racial identity and working for racial justice—gave me the best chance of "healing" from the harm racism did to me.

Now, if you're a person of color, you likely have firsthand knowledge of and experience with how racism looks and feels. You are likely the target of racism, and you may experience overt, in-your-face acts of racial discrimination and prejudice such as being called a racial epithet or not having your job application reviewed because you have an "ethnic" name. In addition, as a person of color, you may experience a range of everyday indignities of racism, which Derald Wing Sue (2010) calls microaggressions. These microaggressions—such as Asian American people being asked where they are "from," as if they were not born in the US—can add up over time. Ultimately, as a person of color you can get boxed into stereotypes that have nothing to do with who you actually are, which then puts you at risk for internalizing these stereotypes and believing they are true. Because of these racialized stereotypes, you may be tokenized as the "only" person of color in your school or community, perhaps leading you to believe you have to be overly conscious of being a "good representative" of your race.

The effects of racism may be less clear for you if you are White. Paul Kivel, a White, antiracist author, says White folks indeed benefit from having advantages based on their skin color (Kivel 2011). Because of these advantages you have if you are White, you can be participating in racism, even if it is not overt, because you have internalized these advantages as being "normal" experiences that everyone has. For instance, because you are White, you don't have to experience being called a racial epithet or employment discrimination. However, as White antiracist Frances Kendall (2013) says, there is a cost you as a White person pay for being part of a system of racism—whether you know it or not. When it comes to talking about or challenging racism, you can often feel shame, guilt, apathy, and an internalized sense of dominance and get frozen in these emotions so you can't talk or act. As a White person, you are likely to have lost your connection to your ethnic group (e.g., Italian, Irish, Russian) and may know little about your cultural backgrounds and history. Furthermore, activists like Tim Wise describe the losses White people have in terms of the opportunity to learn a full history of society that includes the achievements of people of color, and why it is so important to interrogate Whiteness so your perspective of the world is not as limited. This interrogation includes learning not only to relate to the wide variety of racial groups that exist, but also how White privilege disconnects you from your own cultural background and how you can act to challenge racism (Wise 2012).

So again, whether you are a person of color or White, there are many inaccurate messages you can pick up from the world about who you are and who other races are. This workbook is all about taking action to develop strategies you can use to begin the journey of healing from racism.

A GUIDE FOR YOUR JOURNEY: THE RACIAL HEALING WHEEL

Take a look at the Racial Healing Wheel below. Each "spoke" of the wheel—or pie slice—represents a healing strategy you can use in your journey of recovery. Each chapter in this workbook explores one of these healing strategies and contains exercises and techniques you can learn to use to educate, inform, liberate, and transform yourself to bring that aspect of racial healing into your everyday life.

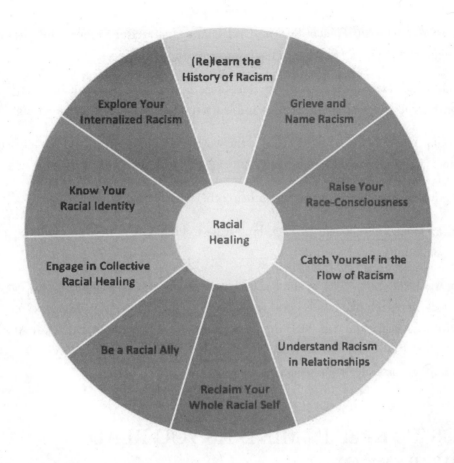

Below is a brief description of each chapter:

1. *Know Your Racial Identity:* Explore what you know about your racial identity and what you were taught (or not taught) about race and racism.

2. *Explore Your Internalized Racism:* Identify belief systems about race and racism that aren't yours, and develop new and more helpful thoughts and feelings.

3. *(Re)learn the History of Racism:* Discover new knowledge and gain a new understanding about racism and how this system of oppression works.

4. *Grieve and Name Racism:* Acknowledge the stages of grief that come with more awareness, learning, and action on racism.

5. *Raise Your Race-Consciousness:* Learn how to act more consciously as a racial being and be a positive influence on others to do the same.

6. *Catch Yourself in the Flow of Racism:* Understand that racism can arise in spontaneous and unexpected ways, and develop skills to interrupt these instances.

7. *Understand Racism in Relationships:* Recognize how racism plays out in interpersonal relationships across a variety of settings and learn to identify when it is happening.

8. *Reclaim Your Whole Racial Self:* Honor the ways you have changed and the authenticity that comes with individual racial healing.

9. *Be a Racial Ally:* Learn ways you can help others and work for racial justice.

10. *Engage in Collective Racial Healing:* Find ways to build circles of accountability and support for community racial healing.

Each of the healing strategies in the Racial Healing Wheel is an important part of your overall healing journey, and each one builds upon the next. That doesn't mean you have to read the workbook from front to back. You can jump in at any point in the workbook to explore and practice a particular healing strategy. If you do read it from start to finish, you might decide to go back and further develop one or more of the strategies.

THINGS TO KEEP IN MIND AS YOU READ THIS WORKBOOK

I'd like to highlight some key points before you begin. First, I call the exercises in each chapter "Racial Healing Practices" for a reason. Each practice builds your strength and prepares you to loosen racism's grip on you and ultimately be able to challenge systems of racism more effectively. You can download worksheets for these Racial Healing Practices from the website for this book: http://www .newharbinger.com/42709. (See the very back of this book for more details.)

Second, as you read through the chapters and engage in the exercises, you'll note that I use the terms "people of color" and "White people." I use a binary system of race (people of color, White) for now, as perceived skin color still defines so much of what we experience in the world of racism. Again, this is shorthand and not perfect, but it allows me to convey the general meanings of who has power and who does not as we explore racism, race, and the journey of racial healing. Keep in mind that in today's day and age, there are *way* more complex racial identities and experiences you may have than the two categories I'm using would imply. You may be a person of color, but are perceived to be White due to lighter skin color. Or, the opposite may be true and you are White, but are perceived to be a person of color because you have darker skin. "Mixed race," "multiracial," "biracial," and other words may more accurately capture your experience—and that is awesome.

More racial combinations exist within families and communities now than ever before, which can also complicate how you experienced your race growing up. For instance, you may be a person of color who grew up in a racially blended family, neighborhood, school, and/or religious/spiritual community. You could be a White person who grew up in a predominantly and historically Black community. You could be Latinx and from a wealthy family, where your class privilege helped buffer some of the effects of racism. You may also have other identities that impact how you experienced your race, as you will explore in chapter 8. Our experiences and identities of race can get very complicated. You may have racial privilege but a lack of privilege based on your other identities, or vice versa—and this means that the work you'll do to heal will be unique to you.

Third, regardless of your particular mix of identities regarding privilege and oppression, the majority of the healing practices involve reflecting on your *own* experience of race and racial identity. You might choose to use the words that are most empowering for you, and even cross out the words I use if they are not helpful to your understandings. And if some aspect of racial experience I describe doesn't sound like your own, know that this workbook will give you lots of opportunities to explore these intersections and get busy with your own unique racial healing work.

Finally, be gentle with yourself as you embark on this part of your racial healing journey. You may have thought about racism a lot, rarely, or somewhere in between. You may have done some racial healing—investigating your history with racism and how it affects your thinking and the world—and then forgotten about it, and restarted, or you might never have contemplated it at all. As you work through this book, you may whiz through each chapter, or you might need to take your time, or need to take breaks to let things digest. You may read alone or gather with fellow comrades who are also committed to healing from racism. You may struggle along the way (especially because racism is unrelenting), but remember that *you* can be in charge of your healing from racism. Sometimes the struggle means you are on the verge of generating a new healing strategy and integrating it deeper into your core understandings of yourself. Any and all experiences you have had about race and racism are welcome in these pages—and, even more so, are critical to your healing and the healing of the world, which truly needs to recover from racism. And remember that no matter how you choose to do this part of your journey, embody it with gentle compassion and curiosity. Racism is as impersonal as it is personal, and just when you think you "have" it in terms of understanding, the next moments can feel like you don't know anything and that racism is just simply impossible to heal from and overcome. So take time to breathe and feel as you work through these pages—it will deepen your work and strengthen your resolve to continue doing the work you *can* do as an individual to challenge racism and do some healing in the process.

THE JOURNEY BEGINS

Healing from racism is a journey. This journey starts with reflecting on what you, as a White person or a person of color, have been taught to believe about the world and your own race. This journey can be a bumpy ride, as it entails relearning the history of the world and how racism came into practice, as well as understanding how this history is linked to racial myths and stereotypes that you have been taught to believe. In so many ways, to heal from racism, you have to reeducate yourself and unlearn the processes by which racism thrives—that is, how racism is internalized for people of color and how race, ethnicity, and Whiteness are made to be invisible for White people.

This workbook breaks new ground by giving you tools that will help you as a person of color or as a White person to heal from the harm of racism you've faced or done and encourage others to heal from racism in the same way. As you work through the exercises in each chapter, you will explore your own race from an intentional perspective of healing, transformation, and liberation, while also learning about the possibilities for healing for other racial groups.

A good place to start is by exploring your own racial identity and experiences—which we'll do in chapter 1.

CHAPTER 1

Know Your Racial Identity

To understand how racism works, it's important to know about your racial identity and your racial identity development. *Racial identity* is a social construct that generally refers to a group that is thought to share a racial heritage. For example, my dad was Indian, so he shared a racial heritage with Indians and South Asians. Meanwhile, your *racial identity development* refers to the stages or processes you experience in learning about your racial identity. As my dad's racial identity unfolded over time, he went from being oblivious to what it meant to be South Asian to realizing—as a result of a critical incident of racism—what his race was and that racism was a real thing that exists. To deal with this, he then immersed himself in South Asian circles and communities, deriving comfort, validation, and shared experiences related to his race. Later, he came to view people who weren't South Asian as people with whom he could also form safer communities. Ultimately, through his racial identity development, he learned what it meant to have and claim an Indian racial identity.

When it comes to your race, developing a positive racial identity is important (Neville and Cross 2017). A positive racial identity means you are secure in your racial identity, you are aware of the history of your racial group, and you are able to identify when you are being racially stereotyped. Notice that having a positive racial identity is very different from having an identity under White supremacy, an unjust system where one race is inferior to another. Rather, a positive racial identity means you have spent time learning about who you are as a racial being—both the privileges and the disadvantages it affords you—and how your racial identity affects your experience of others and the world.

Developing a positive racial identity entails cultivating nonjudgmental curiosity as you learn about your racial identity. This may seem like a simple thing, but curiosity is one of the most challenging of human emotions to cultivate when it comes to race. Ultimately, being curious about your race and racial identity development means that you question old ideas, remain open to new ones, and see what information best fits you—and you keep cultivating that curiosity over time.

At the same time, it can be especially challenging to be curious when you feel stressed, anxious, worried, sad, frustrated, or angry, which are just a handful of the emotions you may feel as you learn more about race and begin an intentional healing journey from racism. So think about curiosity as a muscle that you need to develop and strengthen in order to be able to breathe. Without this muscle, your lungs can't expand to receive new air; with this muscle, you are able to release the old and let in the new.

Let's use your curiosity muscle to investigate some of the earliest things you learned about race and racism, of which racial identity is one aspect. Here, we'll embark on our first Racial Healing Practice. (As a reminder, all of the Racial Healing Practices can be downloaded from the book's website at http://www.newharbinger.com/42709.) For this and each exercise you do in this workbook, write the first things that come to mind. Don't analyze. Let your first responses guide you, as they are usually the most truthful—and most vulnerable—parts of your experience.

RACIAL HEALING PRACTICE
My Earliest Memories of Race and Racism

Think back to the earliest time you realized you had a racial identity. It's okay if you don't remember all the exact details. Describe as much as you can about that experience here.

Starting Kindregatten in T'dad at Holy Family + having a girl come + ask me my name + + when I said it, she couldn't understand + said I spoke funny.

What did this experience teach you to think about your own race? Write about those *thoughts* here.

That I was different. Out of place. I had just moved to T'dad from Jamaica.

Thinking about this earliest time you realized you had a racial identity, write about the *feelings* you have as you remember this experience here.

I was sad from the move + very sad + frustrated that I had to say my name so many times. But once she got my name, we became best friends.

As you explored your earliest recollection of race, what stood out the most for you? Was there anything that surprised you as you wrote about your earliest memories of your racial identity? You might notice a common theme in your recollection that connects to thoughts and feelings that still linger about race and racism today. The feelings that come could be surprisingly negative or positive. For example, you might have felt shame, guilt, and embarrassment writing about these memories—or you might have surprised yourself by remembering a time you experienced pride in your racial identity. No matter what feelings came up, hang on to your curiosity and build that muscle as we delve a little deeper into why those earliest memories matter.

One of the most helpful ways to develop your racial curiosity muscle is to swap and share stories with other people who share your racial identity and others who are of a different race so you can notice how common the experiences and feelings are that people have about race and what they learned growing up. Check out Phillip's story below about his earliest memories of being White and the feelings that came up for him remembering them.

Phillip's Story: "I Don't Like Those People"

The first time I can remember thinking about race was when I was three or four years old. I was in the car with my mom. She was driving us to my grandma's house, and we were driving on a different road than usual. Along that road were several neighborhoods where Black people lived. I said out loud to my mom, "I don't like those people." I feel a lot of emotions remembering that story, mostly shame.

When I talked about that story with my mom recently, she remembers being shocked when I said that. She wondered where I had "gotten that type of thinking," because according to her she didn't teach me that. She's right. She never taught me to say something like that. But somehow I had picked up that thinking somewhere.

If you are White, Phillip's story may resonate with you. Even if no one is "teaching" them to be racist per se, little children are like sponges and pick up that thinking from the world in which they live. It's common to feel ashamed of those thoughts learned from society, and it can feel like you should have known better, done better, and figured out some other way to think and be around race.

If you are a person of color, Phillip's story may bring up emotions too—anger, irritation, the feeling of suspicion confirmed—but you may not be surprised. You may know all too well that racism is taught in covert ways that are hard to identify. Read Della's story below to see how she remembered her earliest memories of being Latinx.

Della's Story: "I Wish I Didn't Want to Be White"

I think I was four or five years old when I realized I was Latina. My parents moved from California to Connecticut. There were two other people of color in my grade, both African American. I remember being called a word I don't like to repeat. I didn't know what it was, but my whole body knew it was bad. I ended up getting a stomachache that day and going home. My mom kept asking me if anything had happened that day. Later on that night, I asked her what that word meant. She told me it was a bad word and not to worry about it. She told me to be proud of who I was and my background. She even told me stories about our family and how many accomplishments they had made. But that night when I went to bed, my stomachache turned into feelings of anger. I wished I was White, and then I felt like that was wrong too. I was so confused. Remembering this, I feel a lot of shame. I wish I didn't want to be White when I was young. It's like I turned my back on my culture without even knowing it and didn't have words to describe what was happening.

When it comes to her earliest recollections of race, Della's story is very different from Phillip's in some ways. At some point in his life, Phillip learned to categorize people of color as different from White people like him, and he learned that this difference was not to be liked. As for Della, she learned she was different racially from White people—and she learned to internalize that difference as something that was not as good about her own race. However, both stories share the feelings of shame. I would even say they share feelings of confusion. These feelings of confusion came for both Phillip and Della because there was information they needed about race and racism that they just didn't have at that point in their lives. For instance, knowing that different races not only exist but also are valuable, and that all people are worthy of respect regardless of their race, would have been helpful to both of them.

Somehow, Phillip and Della didn't get these explicit positive messages from their families, school textbooks, and other sources of information. This could be for a multitude of reasons. Their parents may have been taught to not trust, like, or engage with people of another race. Or it may have been because racial identity and its stages aren't typically included in school learning; often, schools use a "we are all the same" approach to race instead, disregarding the current realities of racism. No matter the reason, in the absence of positive information about people of color and in the context of White supremacy, it is not surprising Phillip and Della would internalize racially stereotyped messages about who they and other races were—and come to act on those messages, whether by disparaging people of other racial identities or disparaging their own.

Now, we could blame their parents, families, schools, communities, neighborhoods, and more. But one of the ideas you will learn in this workbook is that a blame strategy doesn't do much for racial healing, and neither does shame, whether you are shaming others or yourself about race and racism. Blame, shame—and let's throw guilt in there too—are some of the mechanisms of racism that actually result in nonhealing responses like inaction, confusion, hopelessness, and feeling overwhelmed. Instead of exploring what the blame, shame, and guilt is about when it comes to race and taking action based on these emotions (e.g., reflecting on how you internalized a racialized stereotype, and doing your best to act differently), it can be easy to get stuck in those emotions, retreat, and hide from a more fruitful exploration of race. As Derald Wing Sue (personal communication, February 6, 2018), Chinese American and multicultural scholar, shared:

> My work on racial/cultural identity development has always been about asking one question: "Why should I feel ashamed of who and what I am?" Asking that question was very liberating for me because I realized I did not have to accept society's inferior definition of my racial/ cultural group. It took a while for me to overcome that cultural conditioning.

This goes back to why curiosity is so important. Yes, these sometimes icky feelings of shame, blame, and guilt will come up as you learn more about who you are as a racial being. The healing-from-racism response I want you to take is to be curious and let that curiosity lead you to action, such as educating yourself on a racial issue or apologizing for expressing a racialized stereotype. Speaking of action, reflect on your answers to the previous healing exercise and do the following Racial Healing Practice.

RACIAL HEALING PRACTICE
Identifying What I Needed to Know About My
Race Growing Up

Reflect on your earliest memories of your own race and racism. List the things you
needed to know to understand race and racism in a more complete way.

1. _____Dad + mom (He proposed to someone else_____
2. _____my hair_____
3. _____Sames_____
4. _____Going to Holy Family meeting Jennelly_____
5. _____

How would knowing these things have changed your earliest memories of race and
racism?

_____

_____

_____

_____

_____

_____

_____

_____

_____

How did it feel to write the things you needed to know more about to understand race and racism as you were growing up? What realizations did you have about what you needed way back then that might apply to what you need right now as you begin a racial healing journey? Remember, no judgment of yourself in this process of exploring, just lots of curiosity. Let's use that curiosity to learn about racial identity development and how your own racial identity development has happened (and can and will continue to happen) over time.

UNDERSTANDING YOUR RACIAL IDENTITY

Scholars like Janet Helms (1990) have studied racial development for several decades now. What we have learned so far is that racial identity development is a developmental process. It starts from an early age (which is why I asked you to explore your earliest memories) and continues to develop as you move through different parts of your life—school, work, family building, developing friendships, growing older, and so on.

Helms (1990) noted that people of color will commonly begin this process before White people, as they are more often asked to confront race and how racism affects them. Her research also demonstrated that while racial identity development is distinct for people of color and White people, there are also some similarities. Helms used to call these developmental processes "stages" or "statuses," but she realized in her studies that racial identity development is not always linear. So, she began using the term "schemas" to describe these distinct developmental moments that you might cycle through and re-cycle through. You'll read about these distinct—and somewhat overlapping—racial identity development schemas below for people of color and White people. As you read, notice the differences and similarities in both and that having a positive sense of yourself as a racial being is a good thing for White people and people of color alike. This is because, as you will see when you look at a racial identity development model, it increases your ability to act more consciously as a racial being. Put on your studious hat for a moment and read the next two sections about the racial identity development processes for White people and people of color. If you're multiracial, you might resonate with aspects of both of these racial identity development processes.

Racial Identity Development: White People

The schemas of racial identity development for White people are conformity, acceptance, resistance, retreat, emergence, and integrative awareness (Helms 1990). Let's look at what each of these developmental moments involves.

CONFORMITY

If you are White, before critical incidents of racism open your eyes to the realities of race in the world, you are fairly oblivious about your race and the race of others. That makes sense, because racism isn't a system that demands to be known, learned about, and questioned. Otherwise, you might have learned about your race and racial identity development in school, or some similar context. You tend to not be aware that racism exists. Sure, you might be able to point out overt acts of racism, or historical ones, and say these are bad. However, in this part of your identity development, you tend to believe the world for the most part doesn't "see" race. You have a "color blind" view of the world with a conformity to White norms, values, and ways of doing things that is unquestioned. *Feelings in this schema include obliviousness, safety, contentment, satisfaction, and comfort.*

ACCEPTANCE

As a White person in this schema, you more consciously reject the notion that racism is real. When people of color talk about racism, you dismiss their thoughts and feelings and justify your own position that racism isn't an issue. It's tough for you to see the racism in whatever topic people of color are bringing up. You urge people of color to assimilate and merge with the (unacknowledged) White norms in whatever setting they are in so people of color stop "causing problems." *Feelings include alarm, surprise, anger, anxiety, and being overwhelmed.*

RESISTANCE

In this schema you begin to distance yourself as a White person from the idea that racism is real. It's too difficult to think about racism. You might have tried to address some issues of racism and gotten criticized by White allies (White people who are antiracists, which you'll read about in chapter 9) or people of color. The persistent and exhausting nature of racism as a system can feel like too much to think about, so you ask questions like "What can I really do anyway?" You tell yourself that racism existed so long ago, and people of all races just need to get along better. You move from minimizing what people of color experience to blaming people of color for racial disharmony. *Feelings include anxiety, anger, worry, irritability, frustration, and numbing.*

RETREAT

If, as a White person, you keep developing your identity through paying attention to race, you can start to notice that the world is more unfair than you thought it to be when it comes to race. You notice not only that racism does exist, but also how you may have participated in or witnessed racism without taking action. As you explore how this White privilege thing works, and how people of color don't have the same privileges, you move from being unaware of racism's operation in the world to feeling guilty about racism. You can also retreat from fellow White people who are in earlier schemas involving unconscious and conscious denials of the impact of racism on people of color. *Feelings include guilt, shame, anxiety, sadness, hopelessness, and impatience.*

EMERGENCE

As you explore White privilege, you move into taking action about racism, such as starting to educate yourself on what you can do about racism or speaking up when you see a racist incident. You can get stuck, feeling uncomfortable in moments when you encounter your White privilege and then moving on to something less awkward or painful instead of taking action against racism. This is why, to start to develop a positive White racial identity, you need to link up with other White folks exploring racism and broaden your communities to include people from different racial backgrounds. *Feelings include relief, motivation, curiosity, hopefulness, understanding, caring, and grief.*

INTEGRATIVE AWARENESS

In this schema, you continue to look at your White privilege. You also become more curious about other identities you have (e.g., gender, sexual orientation, disability, and social class, which you will explore in chapter 8). You realize the fullness of your racial identity development and the possibility of cycling into other schemas with awareness and skills to experience those schemas more consciously. You have respect for the racial identity development of people of color, including the various schemas they may be in that are different from or similar to your own. *Feelings include a range of healthy emotions related to racism, such as confidence, clarity, curiosity, and motivation, as well as difficult emotions including anger, sadness, anxiety, and fear. You'll sometimes feel these multiple emotions all at the same time in this schema, but you aren't overwhelmed by them so much that you lose your center.*

As you read about White racial identity development, you can see that positive racial identity entails White people realizing that being White in itself isn't a bad thing or a thing to feel guilty about. Yes, when White folks enact conscious and unconscious racism, that is something to feel bad about and to change. But if you get stuck in these emotions as a White person, you can't challenge yourself to learn and grow. White people with positive racial identities understand their White privilege and are more aware of how racism works in the world. They can connect with people from diverse racial backgrounds, and they can use their privilege to take action interrupting and challenging racism.

Racial Identity Development: People of Color

As you read about racial identity development for people of color—conformity, dissonance, immersion, emersion, internalization, and integrated awareness (Helms 1990, Hoffman and Hoffman 2004)—you'll see that the "first" and "last" schemas are the same as those for White people, but the experiences are different, even at those points, because people of color are the targets of racism. You'll also notice the difference in the "middle" schemas that occur as people of color accept that racism is real and move into more conscious awareness of this.

CONFORMITY

In this schema, as a person of color, you are oblivious to the existence of racism. You ascribe to White norms, values, and behaviors without question, thinking that this is just part of being a good person. Some of your emulation of Whiteness is driven by norms that value Whiteness over people of color. In other words, you think White norms are positive and good. *Feelings include obliviousness, safety, contentment, satisfaction, and comfort.*

DISSONANCE

As a person of color, you experience one or more critical incidents of racism and realize the world isn't fair or equitable when it comes to race. For instance, you experience racism yourself. You ask yourself a series of questions: *Did that really happen? Was that directed toward me? Wait—I am a good person, why would they treat me that way?* The experience is not only shocking, unexpected, and unfair, but it also seeds your suspicions of the motivations of White people. As a person of color, you begin to see the world differently in terms of race. *Feelings include confusion, surprise, and anger.*

IMMERSION

Immersion is the schema where, as you notice more and more of the racial inequities you and other people of color experience, you feel anger toward White people. You don't feel as safe being around White people because you can't trust them. You assume that all White people are racist. *Feelings include disillusionment, frustration, anger, and worry.*

EMERSION

Emersion is the schema where you become engrossed in your own racial community due to the distrust you have toward White people in the immersion schema. You experience an even greater need to connect with members of your own race and other people of color so you can feel comforted and validated when you do experience racism. You avoid White-majority spaces when you can and seek community with other people of color. As the target of racism, you may feel the need to be aware that racist incidents can happen and be prepared to act or react. You may seek connection, solace, comfort, and understanding about shared experiences of racism within your own racial groups. You can think of these experiences of racial emersion as healing spaces in which people of color learn strategies for how to cope with racism, stand up against racism, and experience feelings of pride in their race. *Feelings include avoidance, questioning, anger, comfort, and a strong sense of belonging with people of color.*

INTERNALIZATION

In this schema, as a person of color, you have positive experiences with White people who are antiracist and are working to challenge racism in positive ways. You also explore other parts of who you are (e.g., social class, gender, sexual orientation) and how these complex intersections of identity shape your experiences of race. People of color acknowledge they are more than their race. *Feelings include surprise, relief, complexity, and curiosity.*

INTEGRATIVE AWARENESS

At this point in your racial development, as a person of color, you experience the capacity to reach out to a more racially diverse group of people with whom to build communities. You do not feel you are less than another racial group, you are still aware of how racism works, and you value your own racial identity as a part of many important identities you have. *Feelings include a range of emotions related to racism, including confidence, clarity, curiosity, and motivation, as well as anger, sadness, anxiety, and fear. You'll sometimes experience multiple emotions at the same time in this schema, but you aren't overwhelmed by them so much that you lose your center.*

Okay, now that you have read over the racial identity development model for both White people and people of color, take a look at the following figure that includes the racial identity development of White people and people of color side by side. The figure, which was developed by McGrail and Rowe Gorosh (2018), portrays Hoffman and Hoffman's (2004) integrated racial identity development model, which is an adaptation of Janet Helms's (1990) racial identity development models for people of color and White people.

Hoffman Integrated Model

Racial Identity Development

People of Color

White People

confused

disillusioned, angry

Conformity

Dissonance

Acceptance

Immersion

Resistance

identification, belonging

Emersion

Retreat

complex identity

Internalization

Emergence

Integrative Awareness

Take action

Integrative Awareness

understanding white privilege

guilt, shame

blaming reverse racism

dismissive

Conformity

Emulate whiteness

Reproduced with permission from McGrail and Rowe Gorosh (2018)

It's pretty helpful to "see" the schemas laid out like this. Which parts of the figure feel familiar to you and fit your own racial identity development? Which parts do not fit? Notice where the racial identity development of both groups diverge from one another. As you look it over, think honestly with care and compassion about the schema you are in now, and any you have been in the past. Any of the schemas are "good" in that you have thoughts, feelings, and education needs that can support you in moving to greater awareness of your racial identity. Also, the schemas of racial identity development are rarely linear, and it is possible to simultaneously experience more than one part of the model. As a person of color, you can be in the emersion schema and still need to be steeped in the community of color. As a White person, you might be in the retreat schema, or somewhere between acceptance and resistance, and still having difficulty seeing yourself as a person with White privilege—and feeling anger or grief about it.

Keep in mind that racial identity development models are a general starting point for understanding your own racial identity; you might have had very different experiences of coming to understand your racial identity. If you are mixed race, multiracial, or biracial, or describe your race in some other way, the way you experienced race in the world and in treatment from others can make your experiences of race even more complicated. In addition, if you were raised by parents or caregivers of a different race from yours, this can influence the progression of your racial identity development. Joy Hoffman (personal communication January 9, 2019), racial equity educator along with her partner John Hoffman, describes that she is Korean and was adopted by White parents, who had access to White privilege, which gave her lots of access to educational and class privilege as well. Joy reflects that because of this access, her racial idenity development came a little later in life. It wasn't that she didn't expereince racism earlier, but she didn't have the words yet to understand what was happening because she was buffered so much as a Korean American by the Whiteness of her parents. As you read through the next sections about racial identity development for people of color and White folks, pay attention to which parts of the model fit your development or don't. But first, do the next Racial Healing Practice to identify where you are in your own racial identity development.

RACIAL HEALING PRACTICE
Knowing the Twists and Turns of My Racial Identity Development

Take a quick look back at the racial identity development model, and respond to the following prompts. It's okay if you don't have answers for each of the prompts.

Does the racial identity development model mirror your racial development? Which parts of it match your experience? Which do not?

_____

_____

_____

_____

_____

_____

_____

Describe how your life was before you realized race and racism existed.

_____

_____

_____

_____

_____

_____

_____

Describe the first time you saw racism happening (this may be similar to your response in the first Racial Healing Practice in this chapter). Were you the target of the racism, did you enact the racism, or did you witness the racism? Include a description of your thoughts and feelings at the time.

_____

_____

_____

_____

_____

If you are White, describe a time when you felt you were "color blind"—when you tried not to "see" race. If you are a person of color, write about how you coped with realizing that racism was a real thing that you needed to think about a lot. Include a description of your thoughts and feelings at the time.

_____

_____

_____

_____

_____

If you are a person of color, how have people, places, and institutions influenced you in the immersion and emersion schemas? As a White person, how have people, places, and institutions influenced you in the resistance, retreat, and emergence schemas?

_____

_____

_____

_____

_____

If you are a person of color, was there ever a time when you wanted to spend time with your own racial group as a source of empowerment and understanding? If so, write about it. If you are White, describe a time when you started to explore the privileges that came with being White. Include a description of your thoughts and feelings at the time.

_____

_____

_____

_____

_____

Has there been a time when you sought to intentionally build a diverse racial community in your life and felt positively about your racial identity? Include a description of your thoughts and feelings at the time.

_____

_____

_____

_____

_____

_____

Are there other periods of your racial identity development that don't really fit into the racial identity development model—or that seem important to write down to give a fuller picture of how you came to know yourself as a racial being?

_____

_____

_____

_____

_____

Did you notice that some of the prompts in that exercise were easier to respond to than others? That would make sense, as different emotions come along with each of part of the racial identity development model. Did more than one example come to mind for some of the prompts? That would also make sense, as racial identity development isn't a linear process, where one schema happens before the next in a predictable way.

One thing to note about racial identity development is that it is influenced by the world around us. For example, when my Indian dad died (I was in my 20s), as a mixed-race person of color, I felt drawn back into racial identity emersion. I wanted to spend all of my time with South Asian people, and it was in these communities that I found the most comfort. Think about how your racial identity development has been influenced by the experiences you've had, as well as national and international events, people, places, and institutions.

There are a few other things to keep in mind about racial identity development:

- This racial identity development model is just that—one simplified picture of how our racial identities tend to develop. Yes, there is research to support the idea that racial identity development typically proceeds in the schemas outlined (Atkinson, Morten, and Sue 1998; Cross 1991; Helms 1990). It is also true that research can't capture every lived experience of racial identity. Lots of other things can influence your racial identity and matter a lot too. For instance, you may have grown up in a racially homogenous neighborhood and not thought much about your race, much less had a critical incident, until much later in life, such as in college or in your first job. Like my dad, you may have moved from one country to another where a different racial group is in the majority. So getting curious about what other factors, events, or circumstances influence your racial identity development is extremely valuable.

- Remember that the model may "look" linear, but the experience of developing a racial identity often isn't. Even though racial identity development starts early in life, the awareness of what you are feeling in the different parts of the model grows over time and with more experiences. It doesn't just happen from start to finish. You can spend a lot of time in one part of the model or another, and you can move back to an earlier schema of the model depending on current societal events. For example, when a dramatic experience of racism happens, people of color who are in the integrated awareness schema may need to be surrounded by other people of color, therefore moving to the immersion schema. Or White folks, feeling shocked after White nationalist marches and sentiments expressed at the highest levels of our government, may move from integrated awareness into the retreat schema instead of taking action. Everyone has their own racial identity development. And when you consider the fact that folks are typically in different schemas of racial identity development, you can see how lots of misunderstandings, disagreements, debates, and disconnections about race and racism can happen. This is why when racial topics come up at the family holiday table, the conversations may not always go that well. For instance, if you are White and in the integrative awareness schema and one of your White family members is in the retreat and resistance schemas, it may be difficult (or impossible) to get them to reflect on their White privilege. Because people are at different racial identity developmental moments, they may not have the ability to "hear" one another. Instead, you might need to provide them with information (e.g., books, articles) that they can review on their own to expose them to new ideas about race and racism.

- Possibly the most essential and challenging thing to think about is that each part of the racial identity model is an important place to be. It's tough to develop a positive sense of your racial identity without experiencing each schema in the model. For instance, let's say you are a person of color in the first schema, conformity. At this point your experience of racism is one of obliviousness. However, as you move from that schema to dissonance after experiencing critical incidents of racism, you have the opportunity to learn more and more about yourself as a racial being. Then, you get to immerse yourself with other people of color to learn even more about your racial identity. With each developmental progression, you learn different things about yourself as a racial being and about other races—ideally being able to develop a positive sense of racial identity.

When you have a strong racial identity—a sense of your race, the privileges and disadvantages afforded to it, and what you might owe or should come to expect from others as a result—you become more secure, grounded, and aware of your race and how racism works. That gives you the ability to make more informed decisions, think more accurate thoughts, and cultivate communities that can do the same about race and racism.

Before we wrap up this chapter, take a moment to check in with yourself about how you feel about your racial identity right now.

RACIAL HEALING PRACTICE
What Is My Racial Identity Now?

Glance back again at the racial identity development model and respond to the following prompts.

Where would you place yourself in the racial identity development model right now?

_____

_____

Do you need to move into a more positive sense of your racial identity development? If so, what support, experiences, learning, understanding, and so on would you need to do this? Keep in mind that if you're in integrative awareness a good deal of the time, there may still be events, experiences, places, and people you experience that pull you into a different part of the racial identity model.

_____

_____

_____

_____

_____

Describe a recent situation that might have drawn you into an earlier schema of your racial identity development.

_____

_____

_____

_____

_____

How does it feel to write about where your racial identity is now? Did you judge yourself or feel like you should be somewhere you aren't? Or, did you start to feel curious about all the things that might have influenced where you are in your racial identity right now? What did you notice about what you need to develop a more positive racial identity?

As you have been reflecting on your own racial identity, has it been a tough thing to do, or has it come pretty easily? I find at times reflecting on my racial identity can be challenging. For example, even when I am in integrative awareness, I still may have an experience that is tough as a person of color, and suddenly I am in a different part of my racial identity development. It doesn't mean the integrative awareness is gone or that I feel negatively about my racial identity; it just gets a little more complicated because the feelings are so different for each part of racial identity development. I may cycle into obliviousness about race and then be shocked when I encounter racism. Or I might feel I need to be around mostly people of color because of a certain racist national or political event that has happened. It is tempting to judge yourself for these sorts of feelings, but remember, what's most important is to be curious about where you're at with your racial identity and what's influencing that. Then, you can get the support you need to feel secure and positive in your racial identity and move from a place of inaction and unawareness to action and knowledge. That is why knowing about your racial identity is an essential part of your racial healing journey.

RACIAL HEALING WRAP-UP

You started off this chapter with exploring your earliest memories of race and racism, and then learned about racial identity. In the process, you discovered the importance of developing a positive racial identity, which, rather than proceeding in a straight line, can be an evolving spiral where you move forward, backward, and sometimes all around the model.

In chapter 2, you will learn more about how your racial identity has been shaped by events, people, family, places, institutions (e.g., schools), neighborhoods, religious/spiritual communities, political affiliations, and other influences, and how racism gets internalized in all of us.

CHAPTER 2

Explore Your Internalized Racism

Now that you know having a racial identity is a good thing, we can think a little more about how racism gets internalized. The template of racism we learn places people of color in an inferior racial position compared to White people. People of color and White people alike absorb this principle; it then informs the way we perceive the world and the way we behave in it. For people of color, internalized racism—the racialized and stereotyped ideas about their race they learn from the world and society—can result in a range of painful emotions and beliefs, stress, ambivalence or even hatred for their own culture, or a sense that life is harder for them for reasons they can't quite explain. For White people, the phrase "internalized dominance" may be more accurate; racism, with its assumption of White supremacy, can lead to ignorance and disregard of other cultures and blindness to their own privilege. There is widespread inability and failure among White people to acknowledge that racism is real, exists, and is a system operating with folks tagged with advantages and disadvantages (with the result that White people may remain in the conformity schema of racial identity development, as you learned in chapter 1).

The internalization of racism is a key mechanism of how this system of oppression works. When you "explore your internalized racism" as one of the spokes in the wheel of racial healing, you are becoming clear about how to know when that internalization is happening, the costs it can have for your mental and physical health and well-being, and how to interrupt it.

RACIAL SOCIALIZATION: HOW YOU LEARN WHAT YOU KNOW ABOUT RACE

Merriam-Webster's dictionary defines "socialization" as the process beginning during childhood by which individuals acquire the values, habits, and attitudes of a society (Merriam-Webster.com, s.v. "socialization"). When you unpack that definition, socialization is essentially how you learn to be a grown-up so you can function in the world.

As for how this happens—especially across the many identities we have—I like to use Harro's (1996) cycle of socialization (below) to understand what socialization is and how it works.

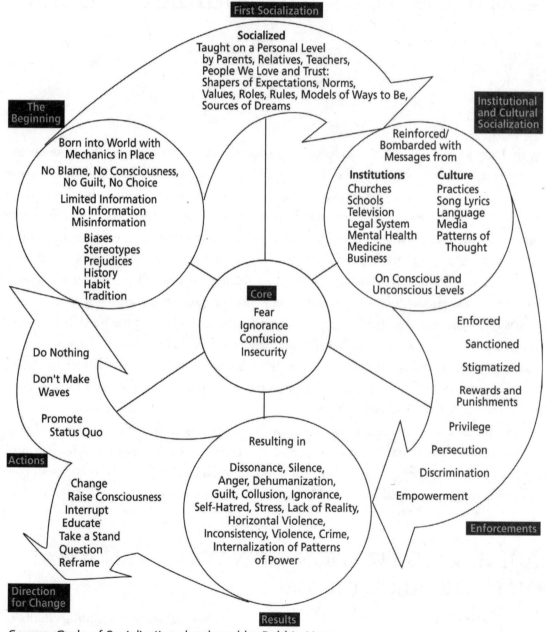

First Socialization

Socialized
Taught on a Personal Level
by Parents, Relatives, Teachers,
People We Love and Trust:
Shapers of Expectations, Norms,
Values, Roles, Rules, Models of Ways to Be,
Sources of Dreams

The Beginning

Born into World with
Mechanics in Place

No Blame, No Consciousness,
No Guilt, No Choice

Limited Information
No Information
Misinformation

Biases
Stereotypes
Prejudices
History
Habit
Tradition

Institutional and Cultural Socialization

Reinforced/
Bombarded with
Messages from

Institutions
Churches
Schools
Television
Legal System
Mental Health
Medicine
Business

Culture
Practices
Song Lyrics
Language
Media
Patterns of
Thought

On Conscious and
Unconscious Levels

Core
Fear
Ignorance
Confusion
Insecurity

Do Nothing

Don't Make
Waves

Promote
Status Quo

Actions

Change
Raise Consciousness
Interrupt
Educate
Take a Stand
Question
Reframe

Direction for Change

Resulting in

Dissonance, Silence,
Anger, Dehumanization,
Guilt, Collusion, Ignorance,
Self-Hatred, Stress, Lack of Reality,
Horizontal Violence,
Inconsistency, Violence, Crime,
Internalization of Patterns
of Power

Enforced

Sanctioned

Stigmatized

Rewards and
Punishments

Privilege

Persecution

Discrimination

Empowerment

Enforcements

Results

Source: Cycle of Socialization developed by Bobbie Harro
© Readings for Diversity and Social Justice, Routledge 2000

You can see that Harro identifies five stages of socialization in her model. The first stage, "The Beginning," refers to the way societal norms are already set in place when we're born. These societal norms provide the belief systems for the second stage, "First Socialization," where we learn from our closest family members how to "be" and "act" in the world according to those societal norms. The third stage is "Institutional and Cultural Socialization," where we enter schools, places of worship, and other community settings and receive similar messages about our identities that reinforce our first socialization. Within these institutional and cultural sites of socialization (as well as our families), the fourth stage, "Enforcements," occurs, as we either get rewarded for staying within societal norms or get punished for stepping outside of those same norms. Finally, in the fifth stage, we embody the "Results" of socialization, which can range from personal feelings and thoughts about our socialization to the ways we navigate society. We continue to manifest these racial socializations until we "wake up" and begin to question each step.

Because I grew up in the South, when I think of the "beginning" and "first socialization" I experienced, I remember being socialized across many of my identities in a specific geographical context. My White mom taught me how to have manners and "good home training" so I would do the right thing when I was out in public. I was also being socialized to wear westernized clothes, to speak without an "accent," and to obey my elders at any cost. On the other hand, my Indian dad—who was socialized in a very different South Asian culture—was training me to be grown up in some similar ways to my mom's training (e.g., say "please" and "thank you," obey your elders), but he wasn't teaching me to say "yes ma'am" and "yes sir," as my mom was. Dad was teaching me that I should live with my brother until I got married (groan, I mean living with my brother??) to a man (I turned out to have a queer identity—surprise!). The point is, of course, as a mixed-race person, my socialization was influenced by a few different cultures.

In addition to socialization by my mom and dad, there was my "institutional and cultural socialization": a combination of the Catholic school I attended and the Sikh religion I was raised in. I said the prayer of St. Francis of Assisi each morning at school; I had my palms together with my hands in a prayer position and my head bowed. When I attended the Sikh *gurudwara* (Sikh house of worship), I sang *shabads* (spiritual songs) and also had my palms together with my hands in a prayer position and head bowed—except I sat on the floor cross-legged, with no shoes, as this was a critical sign of reverence. The "enforcements" came in my family and schools, where I was punished through teasing or bullying because my skin was too dark or the Indian food I brought to school "smelled weird." If I expressed any type of identity other than "straight," I was also verbally harassed. On the other hand, when I tried to "act White" and "straight," I was rewarded and life was a little easier (even though I was faking it big-time). The "results" of this socialization were that I was scared to express my queer identity, and I knew my mixed-race identity wasn't exactly on the "rewards" list—so I just knew deeply that I didn't fit what I had been socialized to be.

So you can see different socializations in my past. It's not always about race; socialization happens around a lot of social identities (see chapter 8). But no matter the identity, my various socializations were definitely about getting trained in how various things should be done to qualify for "adult status." Let's look at how you can apply Harro's cycle of socialization to your racial socialization specifically.

IT'S A CYCLE: DISCOVERING YOUR RACIAL SOCIALIZATION

Again, socialization happens in many realms—but we are going to focus on racial socialization for now. Take a look back at Harro's figure; you'll use this cycle to examine your racial socialization. Let's take a close look at the stages:

1. *The Beginning.* When you are born, racism is already in place. There are clear messages that being White is superior and being a person of color is inferior. So you really don't have a lot of choice about this larger system of racism and its history of stereotyping, prejudices, discrimination, and other thoughts, feelings, and behaviors. The system of racism has already been set in motion in the world.

2. *First Socialization.* Parents, families, loved ones, teachers, and others teach you racial scripts, which basically are the rules of how to be in the world, in conscious and unconscious ways, as a racial being within White supremacy. If you are White, maybe you don't learn what it means to be White—for instance, that you benefit from the system of racism in certain ways, like being able to get a job easily or not being harassed in public spaces. You may be actively discouraged from seeing race in others or in the world around you, but for reasons that aren't made clear. If you are a person of color, there can also be a vacuum of information—especially if you were raised in a community of primarily other people of color. But it's also pretty likely you began to learn something from the major players in your life—your parents, your family, figures in your community—about your race and what that meant for you in the world, like how you're expected to behave in public or what you are or aren't entitled to. In this stage, all people learn what the norms are and what expectations to have about race—basically, the unwritten, unspoken, but very obvious racial scripts and rules about how race works in the world (e.g., White people are superior, people of color are inferior), your place in the system, and how you should play out your racial role in larger society.

3. *Institutional and Cultural Socialization.* Your first racial socializations are reinforced by the institutions you attend, such as school, and through your culture, such as the language used

or not used in your racial group or in other groups you may be part of. Such institutional and cultural socialization happens consciously and unconsciously with explicit and implicit messages about your race and the race of others. You may be socialized to be proud of your race or to ignore race completely. White privilege may mean you can be oblivious to race and racism most of the time—you don't find yourself acutely aware of your racial identity as you move through the world or worry about how you'll be received because of it. Being a person of color, on the other hand, may mean you experience people seeing you and treating you according to societal racial scripts assigned to your racial identity. These scripts can clash with the ones you've learned from your family. For instance, a Black family may teach their children the value and importance of being Black, yet when their children consume media, they may pick up different messages that being Black is not as good as being White. And there are various coping methods you might use in response. Some of these methods are adaptive (e.g. feeling angry, setting boundaries), and some may be maladaptive (e.g., pretending racism doesn't exist or that racism you experience doesn't affect you).

4. *Enforcements.* In this stage of the cycle, you experience within your personal and other networks (e.g., school, work) the rewards and punishments of the system of racism. The rewards may mean when you don't challenge racism, you don't experience distress and you get to feel like you "belong" with people because you didn't rock the boat and challenge racist social norms. The punishments could include rejection when you do rock the boat. You might lose a friend or family group if you object to a racist comment or act by a loved one; or you might get fired from a job for speaking up or calling attention to racism you experience or witness in the workplace. People of color often experience ongoing racial discrimination, stigma, and prejudice when they try to find work or housing or just be in the world, and they use the range of racial coping strategies they were taught in earlier stages of socialization to cope (e.g., fight back, get angry, pretend it is not happening). White people also experience reinforcement by the system, but their privilege related to being White in the world may be so sanctioned and reinforced that it is not readily apparent and therefore challenging to see.

5. *Results.* As the cycle of racial socialization continues, you act on and perpetuate racialized societal scripts—believing stereotypes you encounter about other racial groups; shaping your behavior to match what you feel is expected of your racial group; enduring poor treatment you receive because of your racial identity. You may be largely ignorant of what is happening in society with race and racism, or dimly aware of and feeling guilty about it, or fully cognizant of it and feeling stressed. You might also experience overt results of racism, such as harassment, violence, and systemic racism, and covert processes of racism, such as others' pretending there isn't a problem of racism in society (which amounts to complicity in racism).

My White friend Jenna received a pretty intense racial socialization. She was born into a world of White supremacy where she had advantages. While her parents never explicitly said people of color were less valuable than her White family, they did discourage her from having friends of color over to her house. Her family didn't have any people of color as friends either—sending an implicit message that being White was different from, and superior to, being a person of color. Jenna went to majority White schools, where she heard people behave in racist ways. Latinx and Asian Americans were "foreigners" and didn't "belong" here, and being fearful of Black people was considered normal. Moving from the beginning, first socialization, and institutional and cultural socializations, she was rewarded for not questioning these ideas growing up because she "didn't cause a fuss" in her family, friendships, or school settings. The results of her socialization, however, were painful for her. She didn't get to develop close relationships with people from different racial groups, and she knew deep inside a lot of the racism she was seeing—even if it was covert—was wrong. So you could say that being socialized as a White person who didn't exactly endorse racism but also didn't stand up to it messed with her head quite a bit.

My friend Ajei, who is Native American, went through the same stages of racial socialization as an indigenous person with some similar effects—but some entirely different ones, too. Racism and White supremacy were certainly in place before she was born; her tribal lands had been stolen many generations ago, so her family was restricted to the US-designated "reservation." In her first socialization, her family taught her not to trust White people, who were often the teachers in her schools. The schools on her reservation used books that barely scratched the surface when it came to the history of her tribe, so her institutional socialization was within a White and Western frame. But she was receiving cultural socialization about what it meant to be Navaho in her community, and she loved participating in tribal celebrations and traditions. There were various enforcements in these contexts, in the form of rewards and punishments. Ajei excelled in school, and she was rewarded for learning and regurgitating the knowledge from her White and Western textbooks. When she questioned some of her teachers' lack of knowledge of Navaho culture and traditions, she was told these were things she would "learn outside of school"—meaning outside of that context. When she left the reservation, she worried about being stopped by the police and harassed by White people in a neighboring community who would talk about her Navaho community in negative ways (e.g., "You are a good Navaho; the others, you can't trust"). The results of her racial socialization left her with anger, confusion, guilt, sadness, sometimes happiness and comfort, and other conflicting emotions about her own race in a White-dominated world.

As you read through the cycle of socialization above and the stories of Jenna and Ajei, you might have seen your own experience mirrored in these stages. Let's explore your racial socialization in an exercise.

RACIAL HEALING PRACTICE
What Is My Cycle of Racial Socialization?

Respond to the following prompts to explore your stages of racial socialization. It's okay if you don't know a lot about your early socialization. In those cases, write about your best guesses of what those racial scripts were.

The Beginning—When you are born, racial scripts have already been laid out in the world, and those who raise you carry them out. Write about the racial scripts the people who raised you were operating on.

_____

_____

_____

_____

_____

_____

First Socialization—Loved ones and others you are around teach you the typically unwritten and unspoken rules about racial scripts. Racial scripts can also be delivered explicitly through verbal messages about your race or other races. Even the absence of exposure to other races serves as a message. Write about the expectations and norms of racial scripts you were taught.

_____

_____

_____

_____

_____

_____

Institutional and Cultural Socialization—Moving outside the circle of people who raised you, you learn about racial scripts from schools, places of worship, health care systems, government systems, and other settings. And you learn racial scripts from your culture, such as the media and culture-specific practices within your cultural group. Write about the conscious and unconscious messages you learned from your racial scripts.

_____

_____

_____

_____

_____

_____

_____

_____

Enforcements—You receive rewards for playing along with your racial scripts and punishments for stepping outside of them. Write about how your racial scripts were revised and reinforced through racial privilege, stigma, discrimination, and/or oppression.

_____

_____

_____

_____

_____

_____

_____

_____

Results—You are part of the overall system of racism and experience dehumanization. That dehumanization may look like silence, guilt, anger, self-hatred, and even violence or other patterns of disempowerment. What have you experienced as a result of racism and dehumanization? Write about that here.

_____

_____

_____

_____

_____

_____

_____

As you completed this Racial Healing Practice, what stage of your socialization was easiest to write about and which one was the most challenging to write about? Did your racial socialization happen mostly through unspoken messages and covert teachings, or was it more in-your-face and hard to escape? According to Harro (1996), the core of the cycle of socialization is fueled by the fear, ignorance, confusion, and insecurity you feel as you learn about what your racial identity means in the world. When you feel these emotions, you tend to stop asking questions that would challenge or question racism—they feel too uncomfortable—and fall back into the racial scripts you are expected to enact.

BREAKING OUT OF RACIAL SOCIALIZATION: ACTS OF FREEDOM AND LIBERATION

If racial socialization is the process of learning to be an "adult" in the world of race and racism, then how do you break through some of the ways you have internalized racism? If you look back at Harro's Cycle of Socialization, there actually is an escape clause after stage 5. As Harro describes it, you can either

1. repeat the racial socialization by taking no action, not stirring the pot by questioning or fighting against the system of racial socialization, and refusing to challenge the status quo, or

2. challenge racial socialization through deciding to make a change. First, you set an intention to resist racial socialization and racism by, to the best of your ability, reeducating yourself about how race and racism works (you will explore this process in chapter 3). Then, you can take this new education to reframe old racial stereotypes and belief patterns, which enables you to interrupt racial socialization and patterns in your thinking, feelings, and behaviors.

This workbook is all about the latter, more healing and liberating option: option 2. You learn to restructure your entire racial socialization, entering the integrative awareness schema of racial identity development—where you have a secure and positive sense of your race, understand how racism works, and appreciate other races—and use that new knowledge to act differently in the world and change it. One of my heroes, US Congressional Representative John Lewis of Georgia, often urges people to be "bold, brave, and courageous" and to do what they can "to get in the way."

Of course, if you think back to what you learned in chapter 1 about racial identity development in general for White people and people of color, you know that even if you are in integrative awareness, you can cycle to another part of your racial identity in a heartbeat. You can be cultivating lots of awareness about your racial identity and how racism works in the world, and then something happens. As a White person, you may get called out for making a racially stereotyped assumption—and bam! You feel hurt and retreat into obliviousness, ignoring the fact that racism does exist and that you have White privilege, even if that privilege is not always apparent to you. Or as a person of color, you may end up exhausted by noticing racism in so many parts of your life, so you retreat into obliviousness to just not think about it for a while.

Let's go back to Jenna's and Ajei's racial socialization stories to see what a more positive racial socialization might have looked like. Both could have been born into a world that is confronting the existence of racism (to some extent this is true for many communities and in many places in our world!). Their first socialization and institutional and cultural socialization could have included Jenna's family helping her understand what it means to be White and how to work against White supremacy and Ajei's family addressing what it means to be a person of color in the context of racism and how to really deal with that and challenge her internalized racism. Jenna's and Ajei's schools could have provided them with guidance about race, racism, and racial identity development as well as how to counter racism and engage in making the world a more just place. (To this day, these are rare resources to find in families or schools.) The enforcements for Jenna and Ajei could have been rewards for raising their consciousness about their racial identity, such as receiving encouragement and praise for learning to be an active bystander who can challenge racism when it occurs. Their families, schools, and other institutions could have had a policy of no tolerance of racist ideas and actions. The results could then be confidence, preparedness, and curiosity about their own and other racial groups, with the goal of developing positive racial identities themselves and respect for others' racial identity and human worth.

Complete the next Racial Healing Practice to do some of that intentional restructuring of your racial socialization. Let yourself dig deep in this exercise. This process is part of the road of your racial liberation and healing. So whether you are in an earlier or latter part of your racial identity development, push yourself to identify the parts of your racial socialization that you just gotta question some more to really understand your racial identity and how it influences your way of being in the world and with others.

RACIAL HEALING PRACTICE
Resocializing My Racial Self

In this healing practice, you will go back through the racial socialization model and identify the messages you *needed to hear* to have a more holistic, truthful, and helpful racial socialization.

The Beginning—Write about the world you needed to see, when you were born, in your neighborhood, community, family, and close personal networks regarding race and racism.

_____

_____

_____

_____

_____

_____

_____

First Socialization—Write about what you needed parents, families, loved ones, teachers, and others to teach you about how race works in the world, your place in the system, and how you should play out your racial role in larger society.

_____

_____

_____

_____

_____

_____

_____

Institutional and Cultural Socialization—Write about the messages you needed to hear from the cultures and institutions around you to move beyond the societal racial scripts assigned to your racial identity.

_____

_____

_____

_____

_____

_____

_____

_____

Enforcements—Write about the positive reinforcements you needed from your personal and other networks (e.g., school, work) to be able to comfortably inhabit your racial identity; to identify ongoing racial discrimination, stigma, and prejudice; and to develop a more helpful range of racial coping strategies.

_____

_____

_____

_____

_____

_____

_____

_____

Results—Write about the results there could have been if you had experienced a more holistic, helpful, and truthful racial socialization. Include messages you needed to receive to hold on to your humanity and be a part of eradicating racism and healing from it.

_____

_____

_____

_____

_____

_____

Identify three main messages you learned from your earlier racial socialization that you would like to change right now. For instance, Jenna might write down that she learned racism was something that "good people" avoid—and ignore—when in reality, it's something that all of us, "good" or "bad," are socialized in, capable of, and obligated to challenge. Ajei might write down that she learned her race was something she could affirm and embrace only in certain environments, not something she should be able to inhabit and take pride in anywhere. Write your early racial socialization messages here. Use the additional lines if you want to write more than three.

1. _____

2. _____

3. _____

_____

_____

_____

_____

Next, identify three ways you can shift these earlier racial socialization messages; basically, identify ways you can take a stand, reframe racial stereotypes and belief patterns, reeducate yourself, and interrupt racial socialization and patterns in your thinking, feelings, and behaviors. Ajei might write how she can interrupt and correct any internalized negative messages about being Navaho so that she can embrace being Navaho in different environments. Jenna might write about how she began to use White privilege to take a stand against racism and how she could reframe the subtle and overt racist messages she received from her White family and homogenous school environment about race.

Write the new messages you'd like to put into practice here. Again, there are a few extra lines in case you feel that you are on a roll right now and want to identify more.

1. _____

2. _____

3. _____

_____

_____

_____

_____

_____

How did it feel to reflect on (1) what your racial socialization might have been if it had been carried out in the efforts of ending the system of racism and healing and (2) steps you could take toward that outcome? Did you feel excited, hopeful, motivated and/or sad, lost, angry, worried? Remember that all of these feelings are pretty normal. Interrogating racism requires raising your awareness and knowledge about what it actually is and how it works, not only in the world, but also in your own life.

As you make decisions to change, like in the last part of the previous exercise, and learn new skills to achieve that change, you can feel exhausted, tired, and overwhelmed. It may seem like you'll never be able to "fix" the racism in the world or in your life. But I promise you this. Doing the work of racial healing is way better than doing nothing. Even more so, when you do this work, you put yourself in a long tradition of freedom fighters, rabble-rousers, warriors, and important healers who have used their entire lives to work against racism for their beloved community and the world. Now that's pretty powerful to think about.

RACIAL HEALING WRAP-UP

One of the reasons we don't like to talk about race is because much of what we think we are aware of, believe, think, feel, and do with regard to race is grounded in internalized racism. For White people, this process looks like internalized dominance. Internalized dominance hurts White people, as it is dehumanizing, puts them in a place of inaction about racism, and limits their perspectives and understandings of the world. For people of color, internalized racism also hurts, manifesting in untrue beliefs about their race even if they have been taught by their families and communities to be proud of their race.

Interrogating your internalized racism gives you the opportunity to reexamine your racial socialization and identify new thoughts, beliefs, and actions you want to take about your own race and racism in the world. When you make this shift, you open yourself to new experiences, understanding, and learning about the world of race, such as being able to consider your own race and others beyond racial stereotypes. When you make this shift, you naturally shift your own part of the world and influence others to do the same. From this renewed commitment and understanding of yourself as a racial being, as you read chapter 3 you will learn some things about the history of race and racism that you may never have known before and realize you want to know more about.

CHAPTER 3

(Re)learn the History of Racism

So much of what you learn in your history books about race and racism growing up is inaccurate or incomplete. For instance, you likely learned that Christopher Columbus "discovered" America, when in actuality, he landed in the present-day Bahamas and colonized indigenous people, claiming their native land for Spain (Zinn 2005). He also brutalized the indigenous people and the people who worked for him. You may also not know that Columbus said, "Let us in the name of the Holy Trinity go on sending all the slaves that can be sold" (Burmila 2017). All that's just scratching the surface of his story and the stories of the indigenous people whose trajectories were forever altered by his actions and the White supremacist beliefs that drove them—that his people were superior and indigenous people were inferior, meant to be dominated.

In this chapter, I'll give you a brief overview of the history of racism from colonization practices to the Atlantic Slave Trade and more. There is so much more information we all need to know about the history of race and racism in the world in order to better understand how we got to this point. This chapter won't give you all this (re)education, but key racist events you read about will spur you to make connections from the past to the present. For example, when you know more clearly how racism manifested itself in the early history of the United States, you can start to see the long-lasting effects it still has in this country. Moreover, knowing how these events in the US were connected to racist and colonial contexts around the world will help you understand how racism continues to operate globally. When you use the racial healing strategy of reeducating yourself about the historical markers of racism and how it was first experienced for multiple racial groups in the past, you get to fill gaps in your knowledge about historical racism and its underlying structures—a crucial step in your journey of racial healing.

WHAT YOU LEARNED ABOUT RACISM—AND WHAT YOU DIDN'T

If someone asked you when and where racism started, what would you say? Maybe you learned that racism started with the Atlantic slavery trade (a somewhat "US-centric" idea) and that it was mostly African Americans who experienced this type of racism. Your response might even begin with what you know about your own racial group's history regarding racism. If you are Irish or Italian or identify as a White Jewish person, you might know about the history of your family's immigration and the discrimination they experienced as immigrants, even if you don't experience anything of the kind today. As a person of color, you may have heard stories about your family being targets of racism for many generations (e.g., Native American tribes' land being taken by White "pioneers"; African Americans' past enslavement, discrimination under Jim Crow laws, and current overincarceration; Mexicans' loss of lands during the Mexican-American War; Japanese-American citizens' internment during World War II).

Or maybe you weren't taught anything about the roots of racism. I know I read history books that never used the word "racism," much less talked about how it worked. I had teachers who glossed over racist events, minimizing its lasting impact, like "Yep, bad stuff happened, but it's all in the past." So it's good to pause and reflect on what you learned about the roots of racism in your school, family, and other settings—places of worship, community centers, field trips you took (the institutional and cultural socialization phase of your racial socialization). Do the next Racial Healing Practice to reflect on what you learned about the history of racism growing up.

RACIAL HEALING PRACTICE
What Did I Learn About the History of Racism?

In this healing practice, you will explore how much you were taught about racism and what you learned. Remember, don't think too hard—just write the first things that come to mind.

When did you first hear the word "racism"? Who said the word? Where were you? Write anything else you remember about that time.

_____

_____

_____

_____

_____

_____

_____

What did you learn in your family about the history of racism? If you didn't learn about racism in your family, write how you feel about that here.

_____

_____

_____

_____

_____

_____

_____

What did you learn in your schools about the history of racism? If you didn't learn about racism in school, write how you feel about it here.

_____

_____

_____

_____

_____

_____

_____

_____

Were there other places where you learned about the history of racism? If not, write how you feel about not learning about racism in other places.

_____

_____

_____

_____

_____

_____

_____

_____

_____

You just took a snapshot of what you learned (or didn't learn) in your home, schools, and other places about the historical roots of racism. Did anything surprise you in terms of where most of your historical information came from—or did it feel pretty familiar? How did you feel when you started to reflect on what you were told or not told about the history of racism?

ORIGINS AND EARLY HISTORY OF RACISM

No matter what you learned or didn't learn growing up, the fact is racism is an inherently unjust system that has been around a long time—so long that it makes sense it would be challenging to figure out where it started. In this section, we will review some important ideas that inform the way racism has affected different racial groups in the US. This is a brief overview, so notice which parts of this history you need to learn more about and which historical events you already know.

Racist Ideas Were Developed by Racist People

Ibram X. Kendi (2017a), a history professor at American University, thoroughly researched the origins of racist ideas in the US. He found their roots in the racism and slave trade of early fifteenth century Europe, in which wealthy Muslim trade centers heavily relied on the labor of enslaved Black people in African countries. King John of Portugal sought to acquire this Muslim wealth, so he directed his armies to attack these trade centers, taking over the riches of their production.

In response to criticism of this slave trade economy, racist ideas were created to justify these brutal practices—for instance, that Black people would be "saved" by slavery because they were inferior to Whites in their biology and were not civilized. Basically, White Europeans defined their lives as the "norm" for what it meant to be civilized and labeled the inhabitants of African, Asian, and Latin American countries and Native American tribes as too "savage" to know what was good for them. Thus, racist ideas were used to prop up economies in European lands and the lands that colonial powers invaded. As Kendi (2017b, para 10) notes,

> Time and again, racist ideas have not been born and bred in the cradle of ignorant, hateful, or unpatriotic minds. Time and again, powerful and brilliant men and women have produced racist ideas in order to justify the racist policies of their era, in order to redirect the blame for their era's racial disparities away from those policies and onto Black people.

Kendi is speaking specifically about the African American experience; however, his focus on this history of racist ideas in the US applies to other disadvantaged racial groups as well.

To show how such racist ideas were propagated in the US, Kendi (2017a) points out people like Thomas Jefferson, who authored the Declaration of Independence asserting the "equality" of people, yet was proslavery and "owned" nearly 200 slaves. Jefferson, like many other people in power in colonial societies, believed that people of color weren't fit to rule themselves or be equal to others, but rather to *be* ruled. This racist belief system then allowed people like him to promote a limited interpretation of what "We the people" really meant. People of color (and women) were not believed to be "equal" to White men, but rather inferior to them, and White men like Jefferson made sure that this White supremacist belief was allowed to flourish in society.

This belief continued to shape the experiences of Black people and people of other races in America. For instance, the enslavement of Black people was a driving cause of the Civil War between the North and the South. The southern Confederacy fought for the right to continue slavery, upon which their economy depended and their way of life was *thought* to depend, while northern abolitionists fought to end enslavement practices they recognized as racist, abusive, and immoral. These abolitionists were joined by others who fought the Confederacy in order to keep the Union together, not to end slavery.

Even after the Civil War, during Reconstruction, Black people in the US had limited freedom—they were not able to vote, they were forced into sharecropping without receiving the promised "forty acres and a mule" that would provide them with financial resources to rebuild their lives and communities, and they faced limited opportunities in northern societies still suffused with racism. Racist Jim Crow laws emerged, and the idea of "separate but equal" public spaces was instituted by White people to disenfranchise Black people and ensure they could not access White schools, restaurants, bathrooms, and other societal institutions. Meanwhile, Black people who applied for home loans were discriminated against, so they couldn't benefit from home ownership as White people did.

White supremacy drove these disenfranchisements, holding up the racist belief that Black people are worth less than White people and in need of governance (and rife for exploitation). Again, although Kendi (2018) is focusing on the African American experience in the US, the labor of people of color has historically been seen as a source of profit without a simultaneous valuing of their humanity. For example, in the 1860s, the Chinese railroad workers were "good enough" to provide cheap labor under harsh and unrelenting work conditions, but were always seen as "foreign" and portrayed as the "yellow peril" even as they contributed to the US economy (Lee 2016). Similarly, White people and communities in the US were okay with hiring Mexican braceros (migrant laborers) in the years leading up to and during the World War II (Cohen 2011). This hiring of Mexican workers came to be known as the Bracero Program in the 1942 Mexican Farm Labor Agreement between the US and Mexico. The program promised labor contracts to Mexican migrant workers that guaranteed safe housing, citizenship opportunities, and possibilities of later immigration reform. However, many in the program did not realize the guarantees of safe housing, and the program ended in 1964 with large numbers of the Mexican workers sent back to Mexico after they had long established lives in the US (Cohen 2011).

These examples reinforce Kendi's (2017a) point that racist people continue to intentionally promote racist ideas to disenfranchise people of color. And you can see these racist ideas—that people of color are less than and worth less than White people, and must be governed accordingly—embedded in your families, schools, and other institutions today. For instance, the police shootings of people of color and high rates of incarceration of Black and Latinx people are the result of intentionally racist policies. Some examples include President Reagan's "war on drugs" in the 1980s that relied on publicizing drug use among people of color—especially in Black communities—and virtually ignored drug use in White communities (Alexander 2012). This resulted in racist overtargeting and incarceration of people of color. The racist war on drugs paved the way for what came to be called "broken windows policing": the idea that urban decay encourages a wide range of minor and major criminal offenses and therefore more police presence is required to "fight" this criminality. With these higher rates of policing came a wider scope of offenses for which communities of Black, Latinx, and other people of color could be targeted for arrest. With these focused policing and social control policies in effect, a "law and order" orientation was essentially implemented—with the driving idea that these communities were unable to govern themselves and "bad actors" needed to be weeded out of a population. Meanwhile, federal funds previously allocated for important social support resources (e.g., community health centers) were instead invested in increased police presence.

The aim of these policies was not, for instance, to have racial equity, or we would see different outcomes when it comes to which racial groups are more highly represented in experiences of police violence and in prison. Whether you are White or a person of color, think about how much you know about the birth of racist ideas and policies in the US. Think about your response to what you've just read. Many White people deny that racism still exists at the institutional level. They don't realize that racism has systemic impacts on people. They think racism solely involves individual acts and beliefs, such as calling someone a racial epithet or holding racist attitudes toward a particular racial group. They are good and smart people who somehow do the mental gymnastics to deny that racist societies and policies exist, which allows these folks to not have to confront racist systems and institutions. (If this is something you deal with in your daily life, know that we will talk more about how you can navigate family and other relationships in the context of racism in chapter 7.)

Colonization Is a Practice of Racism

When you look back to the origins of racism as a system, you learn pretty quickly that the roots of racism and White supremacy are in Western colonization practices, namely the labor of non-Western, indigenous people on behalf of those in Western and European cultures. If racism is a big word, system, and concept, so is colonization. Colonization as a system of power, like racism, was based on beliefs and practices of one group's superiority over the other—typically White folks being superior to indigenous peoples of color.

The project of colonization was driven by beliefs that White colonizers had the right to dominate other lands and cultures because of their race (e.g., British, Portuguese, and Spanish colonization of the Americas). Colonizers believed they were better, smarter, and more resourceful than the people they dominated, and they used their powers of dominance to set up a system in which they were in power, with privileges and advantages that were denied to those whose lands they took over. They did this by destroying religious, spiritual, and other cultural practices of indigenous people and instituting White religious, spiritual, and cultural practices in their place (Zinn 2005). For instance, in the US, White colonizers not only stole the land of Native Americans, but also aimed to dismantle their cultural fabric through disallowing them to practice their spirituality and forcing them to adopt Christian belief systems practiced in Europe. And around the world, Black people who were enslaved from countries like Ghana were forced to replace their cultural and spiritual traditions with White, Christian ones.

Colonization has lasting effects that can often seem invisible. That is the power of colonization—over time, the evidence of its brutality can be erased as the colonizers' beliefs and social order are internalized by the colonized, and as colonizers seldom hold themselves accountable for their actions. For instance, Thanksgiving is a pretty big US holiday that is modeled on a "feast" White Plymouth settlers had after their first harvest that they shared with Native American peoples. However, there is little evidence this feast actually occurred. In the telling of the "story" of Thanksgiving, there is also little reference to the intentional decimation of indigenous peoples that White settlers engaged in, or the fact that, if there was a feast at all, its ingredients would have been taken from indigenous land that White settlers believed was there for them to "take": a thoroughly racist idea.

In the end, the historical realities of colonization have been erased over time, and this erasure is validated by our culture. Think about it—Thanksgiving now is a US federal holiday, paired with Christmas and marketed as one of several winter celebrations of family kinship. This serves to further sanitize the brutality involved with stealing of lands and cultural traditions, replacing it with ideas of a large family gathering and meal.

Pretty much all groups of people of color in the US have had some experience of White or Western colonization, yet very few of these racial groups know the extent of the influence of past colonization on their lives today because few are taught much about this history in their schools and families. For instance, members of racial groups that experienced colonization, whether in the US or in their countries of origin, may have internalized White colonizer cultural practices and values, the vestiges of which can still be identified in their cultural groups (e.g., the belief in many Indian American communities today that light skin is more valuable than dark skin). Latinx people also may have been taught to aspire to White ideals of culture, from beauty and skin color to striving to speak "proper English." Think about how much you know or don't know about how colonization practices have influenced people of color in the land we *now* call the US.

Immigrants Were Compelled to Assimilate and Become "White" to Avoid Discrimination

In addition to having been built largely through colonization practices, the US we have come to know has also been created through its immigration policies—the policies that dictate who can enter a country in order to permanently reside there. Except for the original peoples (i.e., Alaska Native, First Nations/Indigenous/Native American people), all other people (or their ancestors) either immigrated here by choice (e.g., coming through Ellis Island)—often seeking work opportunities, for instance on the railroads that were constructed in the US in the 1850s or in factories in the early twentieth century—or were brought to the US by brutal force and enslavement through the East Atlantic Slave Trade.

The racial categories people got funneled into as they immigrated changed over time as more people entered the country. In 1840, the categories were limited to Free White persons, Free Colored persons, and Slaves. In 1850, the categories became White, Black, and Mulatto because a White person who claimed to be a "racial scientist," Josiah Nott, wanted to investigate the lifespan of mixed-race people of African and White heritage (Little 2018). Then, in 1870, racial categories of Chinese and Indian (referring to Native Americans, who were obviously the first inhabitants of the land we now call the US) were added. And eventually, still more categories (Korean, Hawaiian, Vietnamese, and more) were added over time. (Interestingly enough, "Hindu," was added in 1920 to refer to "Asian Indians," regardless of their religious affiliation—another sign that the racial categories we use have always been socially constructed by the people designing racial systems; Little 2018.)

Why does this matter? Well, it's pretty clear from what we've discussed and what we know of the world that people of color who were brought forcibly or immigrated by choice were held against White standards and forced to endure racist enslavement and/or exploitation as they assimilated.

What's less often acknowledged or explored is that light-skinned immigrants, like Jewish, Irish, and Italian people—who had culturally specific traditions, practices, and ways of being in the world— also faced discrimination from White people who considered themselves and their Anglo-Saxon norms the ones that were "properly" American. What's more, David Roediger (2005), author of *Working Toward Whiteness: The Strange Journey from Ellis Island to the Suburbs*, points out that when immigrants with light skin came to the US, they saw the racial dynamic that White supremacy and slavery had created: White = superior and Black = inferior. So, however distinct their cultural backgrounds, Jewish, Irish, and Italian immigrants all encountered the same immense pressure to assimilate to a larger culture of Whiteness for self-preservation. This racial assimilation not only entailed leaving behind their cultural heritages, but also meant pressure to embrace the racist idea that people of color were inferior to those with lighter skin. As a result, immigrants with lighter skin relinquished their cultures to fit in, and they adopted the racist ideas and policies of the US as they "became White."

If you are White, think about how much you know or don't know about your immigrant history. Was your racial identity affected by this pressure to assimilate into the larger category of White? If so, how do you feel about it? Were there costs involved for you or your family?

Immigrants Were Often Labeled "Foreign" or a "Threat"

Just as there was a process of becoming White subsequent to US immigration, there is a related-but-opposite idea in which immigrant groups are considered perpetual foreigners and/or a threat. Not surprisingly, whereas people with light skin were able to assimilate into Whiteness, it has been people of color who have been labeled as not belonging in some way. For example, in the 1850s, Chinese people were recruited to immigrate in order to help construct railroads and other US infrastructure (Lee 2016). However, when the US economy collapsed due to inflation after the Civil War, White people asserted that the Chinese were taking over their industries and jobs. As a result, the intersections of classism and racism fueled racist policies such as the 1882 Chinese Exclusion Act, which for the next sixty years drastically reduced Chinese immigration, driving the idea that the Chinese somehow didn't belong in the US (Lee 2016).

Similarly, during World War II, President Franklin D. Roosevelt issued the racist Executive Order 9066 that forced Japanese Americans—many of whom lived in California—into internment camps (Reeves 2016). The government committed racist infringement of many Japanese Americans' civil rights—including their right to property, to live freely where they choose, and to be recognized as citizens. Similar events happened to Korean Americans and other Asian/Pacific Islander groups. Around the same time, the Mexican Farm Labor Agreement (also known as the Bracero Program) was instituted, which allowed and encouraged migrant workers from Mexico to work on US farmlands to address the shortage of farm labor at the time but which later denied them citizenship (Maze 2016).

The implication of these events is that there are those groups who "belong" in the US, and there are those groups who do not belong and will be perpetually seen as foreign, with their rights as citizens subject to revocation at any time. To this day, for instance, US-born citizens with Asian/Pacific Islander heritage often report being asked by people they meet, "Where were you born?" and "How long have you been in the US?"—indicating this lack of belonging and perpetual foreign-ness. Other groups, such as Middle Eastern immigrants and US citizens with Middle Eastern heritage, are often treated as though they are foreign and/or a threat to people in the US. Arab American women who are Muslim and wear a hijab often experience harassment, even being called "terrorists," and report feeling pressure to assimilate to White conceptions of culture (Wazni and Beckmann 2015).

Understanding many of these assumptions of who is foreign and who belongs in the US requires acknowledging immigration patterns. Those who seek asylum, those who are refugees from war between nation-states, and those who are forced to immigrate for economic reasons may be able to secure citizenship. However, they still may be viewed as not belonging because of their race or heritage—or seen as a burden to the US. For instance, after a dictatorship collapse in the 1980s, Haitians sought immigration to the US and experienced differential laws and treatment compared to lighter-skinned immigrant groups (Danticat 2017). After a 2010 earthquake devastated Haiti, thousands of Haitians were granted temporary protection status in the US, which they lost suddenly in 2018 (Danticat 2017).

This differential treatment based on one's status as a citizen of a particular nation-state makes US borders and federal administrations sites of institutional racism. The current evolving and politically fraught discussion of immigration builds on an equally complex history of who is deemed valuable enough to be a citizen, which has always been tightly linked to race. Taken as an entirety, these immigration events have long-lasting impacts on the racial psyche of the US for both White people and people of color. If you are White, you likely have rarely thought about whether you "belonged" in the US or not. On the other hand, if you are Latinx, Black, or Asian/Pacific Islander, you likely have been forced to think about your foreign-ness. And if you are Native American, you likely have often wondered about how your tribe might have developed without colonization.

Take a moment to do the next Racial Healing Practice to take your pulse about what you are think and feel about these four origins of racism we just reviewed.

RACIAL HEALING PRACTICE
My Own History Lesson Plan for the History of Racism

In the section above, you learned about just four of the many roots of racism in the US: (1) racist ideas were developed by racist people, (2) colonization is a practice of racism, (3) immigrants were compelled to assimilate and become "White" to avoid discrimination, and (4) immigrants were often labeled "foreign" or a "threat." Write about the thoughts, emotions, and questions that are coming up for you about these.

_____

_____

_____

_____

_____

_____

_____

_____

_____

_____

_____

_____

_____

_____

_____

_____

_____

_____

Next, rate yourself on the degree of knowledge you have about the history of racism for the various racial groups below. Use this rating scale:

1 = I know a lot.   2 = I know some things.   3 = I know very little.

_____   Alaska Natives/First Nations/Indigenous Peoples/Native Americans

_____   Asian/Pacific Islander Americans

_____   Black/African Americans

_____   Latinx/o/a/@/Hispanic Americans

_____   Middle Eastern Americans

_____   White/European Americans

Then, respond to the prompts below:

Which groups did you rate most highly with a 1? What do you know and how did you come to learn so much about the historical roots of racism for these groups?

_____

_____

_____

_____

_____

Which groups did you rate the least highly with a 3? What might be some next steps for you to take to learn more about the historical roots of racism for these groups?

_____

_____

_____

_____

_____

_____

Were there any groups you rated 2? If yes, how can you increase your knowledge of these groups to a 1?

_____

_____

_____

_____

_____

_____

_____

_____

How did you rate your own racial group? What are the knowledge gaps you can address?

_____

_____

_____

_____

_____

_____

_____

_____

_____

What was it like tracking your thoughts and feelings about the four origins of racism? Did you notice there are some origins you want to know more about? I hope you had this reaction to each of them. I find I am always learning new things about how racism originated through reading books on this topic and having conversations with others committed to learning how racism began and continues to influence White folks and folks of color. The more you learn about the history of racism, the better you will be able to make the connection between the racist ideas and policies that happened way-back-when and those that exist today. By completing this Racial Healing Practice, you should have a good idea of which knowledge gaps you can address to continue reeducating yourself about the history of racism.

BECOMING YOUR OWN HISTORIAN—LEAVING NOTHING UP TO CHANCE

When you look back on your early learning about the history of racism, you start to notice the specific gaps in your knowledge. As a White person you most likely learned very little about the role of White supremacy in racism, or about the way Whiteness is a construct just like all racial identities. As a person of color, you may notice that you know a good deal about your own racial group's history of racism, but not so much about what other groups have experienced.

Identifying your knowledge gaps is a part of reeducating yourself about the history of race and racism. In a very real sense, you have to become your own history teacher and grade yourself on how much you know about your racial groups and others when it comes to racism. And you have to refine your history lessons to address the knowledge gaps you have and then go on a journey searching for knowledge. For example, you may not know about the many ways Black people resisted enslavement and Jim Crow laws (Vox 2018). History books rarely tell the full stories of Black rebellions against slavery—of people escaping plantations or helping others do the same (e.g., Nat Turner's 1831 Rebellion). Similarly, history books don't tell the story of Horace Tate and other "hidden heroes" who resisted Jim Crow laws through community organizing and advocacy (Walker 2018). These important steps later led to civil rights gains in education as a result of the 1954 Supreme Court decision in Brown v. Board of Education (Walker 2018). It's also rare that we learn how histories of enslavement and Jim Crow laws set the stage for the current racist mass incarceration policies and practices targeting Black and Latinx people of color today. That knowledge can be found in a variety of forms—from books and movies to online platforms and even museums (e.g., Lynching Memorial in Montgomery, Alabama; National Museum of the American Indian in Washington, DC).

You also may not know about the resilience Japanese Americans cultivated during US internment, such as the gardens they grew in the camps, the art they created, and the communities they strengthened (Kuramitsu 1995). Recently, I've been learning more about the Native American resistance to White colonization (Churchill 2002), including the Shawnee Native American leader, Tecumseh, who led fierce resistance movements against the western march of colonization over tribal lands. Growing up, I didn't read in a single history book about Tecumseh, but as I have gained this new knowledge, I can see the deeply cultural and spiritual strategies of these past resistance movements embedded into contemporary indigenous rights movements led by multiple tribes coming together as water protectors at Standing Rock to stop the construction of the Dakota Access Pipeline (Jaina, Orihel, and Ross 2016). In addition, researchers have identified important resiliencies enabling Latinx people to deal with xenophobic and racial stressors, such as family bonds, extended community supports, and shared Latinx cultural traditions (Cordoso 2010). And these are just a few examples. As you learn more and more, you may notice other gaps in your knowledge that you can address. Think of this process as an ongoing one. You don't have to know everything about the history of racism—but those knowledge gaps become a compass for your reeducation.

RACIAL HEALING WRAP-UP

In this chapter, you learned that the history of racism was created and driven by intentionally racist ideas and policies of White supremacy. The system of racism didn't just "happen" to occur because of people's ignorance or lack of knowledge. Knowing this, it becomes even more crucial to know the roots of racism in practicing the healing strategy of reeducating yourself about race and racism. You have the opportunity to become a historian who not only reeducates yourself on this subject, but also makes sure this reeducation is ongoing. There is so much to relearn, so be sure to keep furthering your (re)education.

Speaking of learning, now that you have an idea of how important history is in healing from racism, you'll explore some of the emotions of grief and loss that can come up as you delve more deeply into racism. In doing so, you will learn you can name this grief and move closer to actions against racism that foster your own healing and the healing of others.

CHAPTER 4

Grieve and Name Racism

As you learn about the history of racism and the effects racism has on your life and the lives of others, you are going to experience many feelings related to grief. Some of these feelings you can anticipate. But some of the feelings take you by surprise, and suddenly your gut, throat, shoulders, and other parts of your body seize up with the intensity of the emotions you are feeling. This makes sense. You feel shame, guilt, fear, rage, surprise, and sadness when you start reflecting on the impact of racism on your life and the lives of others. You soon realize the true meaning of what it means to heal from racism—that it's not all a "head game."

In actuality, healing from racism is not just about what you *know* or what you *do*, but also about what you *feel*. Yes, you need to engage in healing strategies you have explored so far in this workbook. Yes, you need to interrogate your internalized racism and enacted racism when it comes to thoughts and behaviors. However, when you start to check in with your emotions that come up when you really do this interrogation, you see that the feelings can go deep—really, really deep. So one of the healing strategies is to take time to feel all the feelings and know what to do with them, when they are happening, and how many of them relate to grief. Grief doesn't only have to do with death; really, it encompasses any type of loss you experience, including losses caused by racism and White supremacy. In this chapter, you'll explore the grief that comes up for you when you name the effects of racism on your life.

CULTURAL AND SOCIAL NORMS OF GRIEF

Before you get too much further into thinking about grief and racism, it's important to acknowledge that grief has a wide variety of cultural and social norms around it. Cultural and social norms are powerfully ingrained in us from childhood, so they're sometimes hard to identify because it's "just what you do" or "just how things are." But exploring your cultural and social norms of grief and loss can help give you insight into how you might name and grieve racism or not want to do so—both of which are completely natural.

Grief is a part of healing from racism, and how we grieve is influenced by our cultures. When I think about the cultural influences on how I grieve, the city in which I was born immediately comes into play. I grew up in New Orleans, where funerals were not stoic events; they were just the opposite. A funeral was seen as a "homecoming" of sorts, with a lot of talking, big expression of emotion, and eating of really good food. From the Sikh, South Asian side of my culture, saying "good-bye" to an important person in our lives included songs of prayer, permission to sob and cry, large community gatherings, and again, lots of food.

As you can see, I grew up with a lot of cultural permission to grieve out loud, to connect with others, and to express my emotions. When I experience grief and loss about racism, I am immediately drawn to connect with others, to get support, and to be vocal. This is helpful in many ways because I get to share my emotions with community. The downside of these cultural norms is that sometimes I don't give myself enough alone time to really process what has just happened. The cultural norms you grew up with might be similar to or really different from what I just described. For you, experiencing grief and loss might have been a more quiet endeavor, or limited to only close family and friends. If so, you might be really good at getting time with yourself to process racism, but it may be more difficult to share your emotions with others and get support. In addition, for many cultures, grief tends to be a one-time event—you experience a loss, move through formal rituals, and then don't talk about it much after that event. If this applies to your culture, you may be tempted to move on pretty quickly from the grief and loss that you and others feel because of racism.

Take a moment in the next Racial Healing Practice to explore the cultural and social norms of grief that you grew up with.

RACIAL HEALING PRACTICE
Cultural and Social Norms of Grief

Think about a recent loss in your life—it can be a death of a person or some other type of loss, such as a friendship ending, a divorce, losing your home or job, or even a natural disaster. Write about that experience below.

_____

_____

_____

_____

_____

_____

_____

_____

_____

_____

_____

_____

_____

_____

Use the following scale to rate the statements below in relation to the level to which you learned, culturally and socially, to accept such a response to an instance of grief and loss like the one you just wrote. By acceptance level, I am not referring to you being "okay" with the grief and loss, but rather to the degree to which it was acceptable or "okay" in your culture and social groups to express grief and loss in the way a particular statement indicates. Then, you will explore how these ratings translate to the particular cultural and social norms of grief and loss you learned growing up.

Very Accepted	Somewhat Accepted	Not Accepted
1	2	3

When I experienced this grief or loss, it was acceptable for me:

_____ to cry or feel depressed

_____ to express anger

_____ to say I was scared

_____ to say I was confused

_____ to say I was in pain

_____ to grieve loudly and with lots of accompanying emotions

_____ to be around lots of people

_____ to take time off of school, work, or other obligations

_____ to take time for myself and be away from people

_____ to ask for help from a family member or friend

_____ to ask for help or see a counselor

_____ to express concern about what was going to happen next

_____ to struggle with what to do next

When you think about this incident of grief or loss and reflect on how you rated the above statements, what do you realize about the cultural and social norms you grew up with when it comes to grief?

_____

_____

_____

_____

_____

_____

_____

We will explore this more in a moment, but first quickly answer this question: What is your inkling about how your cultural and social norms may shape the grief and loss that accompanies instances and systems of racism you encounter?

_____

_____

_____

_____

_____

_____

_____

As you reflected on the cultural and social norms of grief and loss you learned growing up, did you notice unspoken and spoken rules about how you are supposed to grieve? Do you find that you typically break these cultural and social rules, or do you abide by them for the most part? Cultural and social norms are powerfully ingrained in us, so keep reflecting on these norms and how they shape your experience of loss as you read through the next section on the stages of grief and how they relate to healing from racism.

APPLYING THE STAGES OF GRIEF TO THE GRIEF AND LOSS OF RACISM

Researcher Elizabeth Kübler-Ross (Kübler-Ross and Kessler 2014) identified five stages of grief from her studies of people who were terminally ill: (1) denial, (2) anger, (3) bargaining, (4) depression, and (5) acceptance. Kübler-Ross described these stages flowing one after another, constituting a process of grief. However, she and other grief researchers have noted that the grief process isn't always so linear; you can be in one or more stages at the same time. I see these stages of grief in my own life when I am navigating racism, so I've spent a lot of time applying the stages of grief to the process of healing from racism. Read more about the stages of grief below.

Denial

The first stage of grief is denial, where you experience shock and loss of meaning in your life. Denial about racism can look like White folks enacting White supremacy by telling people of color they are "making too much of a deal" about an instance of racism or systemic racism, or not taking action when they hear a friend or family member say something racist about people of color. Denial can also look like people of color with internalized racism numbing feelings to microaggressions or minimizing a coworker's feelings about a racist work incident. I experience this stage when I'm exhausted and just need a break from examining racism's impacts. You can tell you are in denial when you find yourself discounting the possibility that racism is occurring or isolating yourself in some way. Denial may seem like a "bad" word, especially when it comes to healing from racism. But the denial stage in grief can help you prepare for the emotions to come. I'm not saying denial of grief related to racism is "good" or that you should seek to hang out in this emotion. I think of it as a "pause" button that allows you to begin healing from a loss, once enough time has passed for you to begin processing and understanding what you've experienced.

Anger

Anger is the second stage of grief, and it's an emotion that is usually pretty easy to notice. You feel pissed, upset, frustrated, and irritable about racism. Anger can also be expressed in subtle ways that can mimic the denial stage, such as feeling irritable and frustrated but ignoring these emotions or feeling confused about why you are feeling this way. When I am in this stage, I need alone time so I can journal and sort out my thoughts. You may find yourself feeling so irritable or angry that you just need to "shut off" and not think about racism. Kübler-Ross often talked about anger being a source of strength and boundaries. I like this way of thinking of anger as a sign of our boundaries, as in the part of us that says, "Oh, heck no—this is not okay!" Considered this way, the anger that you feel in moments of racism—whether you're learning to resist racism or to avoid enacting it—points to the action you can take to resist it.

Bargaining

The third stage of grief is bargaining, where you ask yourself the "What if…" questions. What if you had done something differently when you saw something racist happen at work? What if you had learned not to dislike your skin color at an early age? What if you knew the perfect thing to do as a White person that would stop a person's racism in their tracks? You experience pain when you grieve, and the bargaining stage brings this pain front and center. You might feel guilt and shame about lost opportunities to act against racism or challenge racism in some way. Bargaining can also look like people of color going back and forth about whether something racist just occurred to them: "Was that racist, or is that just me being too sensitive?" It can be White folks saying, "Well, I think that was racist, but how can I know for sure?" Essentially, you know you are in the bargaining stage when you find yourself going back and forth—even from extreme to extreme—when it comes to something related to racism.

Depression

The fourth stage of grief, depression, may seem like a heavy word when it comes to racism, but I actually think it hits the nail on the metaphorical head. As the stages of grief progress, you are able to feel more and more vulnerable emotions that are underneath the denial, anger, and bargaining— and that's sadness. It makes sense that this stage of grieving racism can feel like it has no end, like it's going to last forever. And there is some truth to that when it comes to racism. Usually when we experience a loss—such as the death of someone we are close with, getting fired from a job, or losing a friendship—it is a single loss related to that person or situation. But with the permanence and systemic nature of racism, it truly is hard to see that racism will end. When I am in this stage, I remember to connect with people who can remind me that, yes, healing from racism is a long journey, but that our individual acts of uncovering our personal internalized racism, resisting structural racism we experience in day-to-day life—the kind of racism that is embedded in the structures and institutions in which we live our lives, like our schools, governments, social programs, and legal systems—and advocating for the end of structural racism in society all make a big difference not only for our lives, but for the generations that come behind us.

Acceptance

The fifth stage of grief is called acceptance—the stage where you know the loss has happened and you can't go back to obliviousness about it. This doesn't mean you have stopped feeling pain or any of the emotions associated with the earlier stages, but you do begin to accept that this is your "new normal." I think this stage is so powerful to explore when it comes to racial healing. When you accept that racism as a system and structure isn't going away, you can also move into action beyond this acceptance. You can design your new normal as being a freedom fighter, either as a White person or person of color. You can interrogate all you have been taught about the world as you explored in chapter 3, and you can create new intentions for your journey in healing from racism.

Acceptance is the stage I would love to say that I live in most of the time, but in truth I think I bounce around the stages quite a bit, as most people do. However, I have become really good at noticing when I am in each stage, which helps me become more effective at challenging racism and externalizing racism within me. And remember, the stages may not be linear. For instance, you may witness racism committed by others and jump past the anger stage to the stage of bargaining, asking questions such as "Maybe that wasn't really racism?" Or when a series of racist events happens—whether on the news or in your own life—you may skip the anger stage or move right into the stage of depression.

Do the next Racial Healing Practice to explore how the five stages of grief show up in your own life when it comes to your journey of healing from racism, and how this can be influenced by your cultural and social norms.

RACIAL HEALING PRACTICE
Applying the Five Stages of Grief to My Experiences with Racism

Think about an experience with racism you have had recently. For White folks, think about a time you enacted racism or witnessed racism. For people of color, think about what it was like for you to experience a racist incident or internalize racist stereotypes about your race. Once you have that incident in your mind, write about it here:

_____

_____

_____

_____

_____

_____

_____

_____

_____

Next, you have the opportunity to identify the emotions, thoughts, and behaviors that typically come up for you in that stage and related cultural and social norms that are important to acknowledge. You will also be able to identify what you needed in these instances in terms of support and connection to enable you to heal from this racism instead of continuing in an uninterrupted cycle of grief:

Denial—What did this stage look like for this incident? What were the accompanying feelings, thoughts, and behaviors?

Feelings: _____

_____

Thoughts: _____

_____

Behaviors: _____

_____

Cultural and social norms in this stage: _____

_____

What support I needed to challenge my own racism or internalized racism when I was in the stage of denial:

_____

_____

_____

_____

Anger—What did this stage look like for this incident? What were the accompanying feelings, thoughts, and behaviors?

Feelings: _____

_____

Thoughts: _____

_____

Behaviors: _____

_____

Cultural and social norms in this stage: _____

_____

What support I needed to challenge my own racism or internalized racism when I was in the stage of anger:

_____

_____

_____

_____

Bargaining—What did this stage look like for this incident? What were the accompanying feelings, thoughts, and behaviors?

Feelings: _____

_____

Thoughts: _____

_____

Behaviors: _____

_____

Cultural and social norms in this stage: _____

_____

What support I needed to challenge my own racism or internalized racism when I was in the stage of bargaining:

_____

_____

_____

_____

Depression—What did this stage look like for this incident? What were the accompanying feelings, thoughts, and behaviors?

Feelings: _____

_____

Thoughts: _____

_____

Behaviors: _____

_____

Cultural and social norms in this stage: _____

_____

What support I needed to challenge my own racism or internalized racism when I was in the stage of depression:

_____

_____

_____

_____

Acceptance—What did this stage look like for this incident? What were the accompanying feelings, thoughts, and behaviors?

Feelings: _____

_____

Thoughts: _____

_____

Behaviors: _____

_____

Cultural and social norms in this stage: _____

_____

What support I needed to challenge my own racism or internalized racism when I was in the stage of acceptance:

_____

_____

_____

_____

Now that you have more deeply explored the stages of grief and their application to enacted racism or internalized racism, what did you learn about yourself? Are there certain stages that you feel more culturally adapted to or familiar with to move through? Are there stages that are more of a struggle for you? Consider repeating this exercise as you move through this workbook. You can practice identifying which stage you are in and learn more readily about what you need when you are in that stage. You can also look back at earlier chapters and repeat this exercise based on your general understanding of racism and particular incidents of racism you have explored.

EXPLORING THE HARD STUFF ABOUT OUR ROLES WITHIN RACISM

Now that you have explored some of the cultural and social norms around grief, the stages of grief, and how these stages apply to racism, it's time to go even deeper into how racism situates you in a particular role and the related grief and loss you experience in this role. The role you have within racism goes directly back to the racial hierarchy set up by White supremacy, where White people are assumed to be superior to people of color and racist systemic structures and individual attitudes are set into place to enforce this racial hierarchy.

Now, it's very tempting to think, *I'm not really affected by racism,* no matter if you are a person of color or are White. However, I would argue that this thinking is part of denial. If you really think about it, it is super-intense to explore, name, and acknowledge the conscious and unconscious roles we have played within racism. It's tempting for me to think I have gotten over racism or I have a good handle on it. I can think, *I've explored my internalized racism and I challenge thoughts about being "less than" White folks. I've also explored my light-skinned privilege and what this affords me compared to those who don't have this privilege, even as I continue to face racism myself.*

And it's true. I have done these things. It is also true that racism is ongoing in our society. I can have a positive racial identity, but all of a sudden someone asks me, "What are you?" or calls a Sikh family member a "terrorist" because they are wearing a turban. In those moments, I am not always so solid in my racial identity. And even if I am feeling solid, I feel lots of emotions that I have to sort out to move on through my day in a grounded way. I'm sharing my personal example to say that you will grieve the losses you have had related to your role in racism (learning whether you are superior or inferior to others). Not only is it okay to grieve these losses, but it is also important to learn to become aware of this grief so we can heal along the way.

Below are just a few examples of how people of color experience grief and loss related to racism:

- Believing you are less valuable as a person of color than White people

- Disliking your physical features that reflect your race

- Not appreciating your physical features that reflect your race (this may seem repetitive of the above bullet, but these are actually two distinct losses when you learn to not appreciate and value your racial features as unique and amazing!)

- Feeling hopeless after experiencing everyday microaggressions

- Feeling scared after experiencing street harassment

- Denying that racism is impacting you

- Minimizing the effects of racism on you

- Going back and forth about whether racism influences your life

And these are a few examples of how White people experience grief and loss related to racism:

- Feeling guilty that you were taught in implicit and/ or explicit ways that you are better than people of color

- Feeling guilty about making a racist comment

- Feeling afraid to make a "mistake" when it comes to racism

- Feeling angry that you have to work on your racism

- Minimizing the dominant role and related privilege that you have in racism

- Fearing challenging another White person's racist attitudes, thoughts, or behaviors

- Going back and forth about whether you can use your White privilege to make social change

- Being so angry about an incident of racism that you get stuck in that anger and don't actually take action to challenge it

In the next Racial Healing Practice, you'll explore your role within racism as a White person or person of color even more.

Grieving the Role I Have Within the System of Racism

How do you really feel about the role you have within the racial hierarchy? What have been the impacts of this on your life in terms of grief and loss? Respond to the questions below to increase your awareness about this grief and loss.

When you think about your role within racism as a person of color or White person, what feelings come up for you?

_____

_____

_____

_____

_____

_____

How are the feelings you listed above related to the stages of grief (denial, anger, bargaining, depression, acceptance)?

_____

_____

_____

_____

_____

Which stage of grief (denial, anger, bargaining, depression, acceptance) is *easier* for you to experience in relation to your role within racism, and why?

_____

_____

_____

_____

_____

_____

Which stage of grief (denial, anger, bargaining, depression, acceptance) is *tougher* for you to experience in relation to your role within racism, and why?

_____

_____

_____

_____

_____

_____

Overall, what have you learned about yourself and your general reactions in the stages of grief (denial, anger, bargaining, depression, acceptance) that can help you on your racial healing journey?

_____

_____

_____

_____

_____

What insights are you taking away from your reflection on grief and loss related to your role within racism? How can these insights help protect you from internalizing further racism and also help you from becoming numb to the fact that racism is something we need to heal from in order to get to a more just world?

RACIAL HEALING WRAP-UP

Grief and loss is tough to talk about—and it's no different when it comes to the losses you experience because of racism. In this chapter, you reflected on how you have experienced grief and loss as a White person or person of color. You considered how cultural and social norms have shaped your experiences of racial grief and loss, and you learned how to apply the five stages of grief to the role you are situated in within the system of race. This exploration of grief and loss is good prep work for the next chapter, where you'll learn to raise your race-consciousness.

CHAPTER 5

Raise Your Race Consciousness

Race-consciousness means that you are aware of how racism works as a system. You have already begun raising your race consciousness by practicing racial healing strategies like exploring internalized racism, relearning the history of racism, and naming related grief and loss. In this chapter, you will learn how to do things that help you claim an antiracist identity, now that you've learned more about your own racial identity and what it means in your life. In doing so, you will end up expanding your knowledge about your race and the race of others.

RACE, RACISM, AND CONSCIOUSNESS-RAISING

Consciousness-raising is one of those big words—and even bigger ideas. It refers to the expansion, growth, and evolution of our awareness. There are many ways to raise your race-consciousness, and I like to categorize those ways into two buckets of strategies:

1. *Education:* You can read books, blogs, and social media posts about your race and the races of others to learn more about people's experiences and broaden your knowledge base, which raises your race-consciousness. You can also further your race-consciousness by watching documentaries, movies, and YouTube videos that provide you with new perspectives about how White supremacy has worked over time in the US and globally.

2. *People:* You can develop relationships with people outside of your race; this exposure and connection can teach you new things about how other people experience the world as racial beings, which raises your race-consciousness. You can also connect with people within your own race who are examining their internalized racism to help increase your ongoing reflection and learning about race and racism.

There are definitely overlaps between these two categories—and with the (re)education you learned about in chapter 3. The main point is to intentionally reflect on how you can build up these two buckets so you can interact with yourself, others, and the world in a more race-conscious way. For instance, one of my favorite books about South Asians in the US is *The Karma of Brown Folk* by Vijay Prasad (2001). This book became a vital source of education and raised my consciousness in ways I never could have expected. I learned more about the history of my South Asian community in the US, which included a complex set of experiences. Yes, I read about the historical racism South Asians experienced, including many material disadvantages and stereotypes held over from the days of slavery and segregation. However, I also learned how South Asians were often positioned as a "model minority" group, and how this positioning is derived from White supremacy. Prasad talks about how South Asians had certainly experienced racism coming into the US, but they did not experience the generational enslavement and subjugation Black Americans had experienced. On the contrary, South Asian immigrants had higher access to education (and often advanced educational degrees) and financial resources, and were often in the middle class or higher before they immigrated to the US. Therefore, the idea that South Asians were a "model minority group" was an artifact of racism. Yet South Asian immigrants have also benefited from the Civil Rights Movement—led by Black Americans, the very community that South Asians are often pitted against. As I have read Prasad's work, I have also had the opportunity to reflect on how British colonization intersected with Indian caste systems, and how, to this day, this drives many in my own South Asian community to internalize and value White, Western cultural values as "proper" or "civilized" at the expense of their own culture. I've sought to put these reflections into action and identify how I can question and interrogate these same values I have internalized. For instance, I've learned to love my brown skin, even though many of my aunties warn me to stay out of the sun for fear of "getting darker." I've learned to grow my own education about Black history and US leaders who fought for civil rights that my own Indian father benefited from, which therefore gave me advantages I now have in education and class.

The next Racial Healing Practice will help you identify the main ways you can raise your race-consciousness in the education and people buckets.

RACIAL HEALING PRACTICE
Raising My Consciousness Through Education and People

In this Racial Healing Practice, write a *P* for *past* and an *N* for *now*, to note the ways you have raised your race-consciousness in the past, and can do more of right now, in the two categories of education and people (if this is tough to identify, that's okay; give it your best shot). There are a few blank spaces where you can add your own ideas within these two buckets.

Education

_____	Books	_____	Podcasts
_____	Movies	_____	TED Talks
_____	Documentaries	_____	Music
_____	Social media	_____	_____
_____	Libraries	_____	_____
_____	Workshops	_____	_____
_____	Conferences		

People

_____	Keynote speakers	_____	Educators
_____	Author book signings	_____	Religious/spiritual leaders
_____	Book clubs	_____	_____
_____	Street activists	_____	_____
_____	Community leaders	_____	_____
_____	Politicians		

What are three steps you have taken with *education* in the past to raise your race-consciousness?

1. _____

2. _____

3. _____

What are three next steps you can take with *education* right now to raise your race-consciousness?

1. _____

2. _____

3. _____

What are three steps you have taken with *people* in the past to raise your race-consciousness?

1. _____

2. _____

3. _____

What are three next steps you can take with *people* right now to raise your race-consciousness?

1. _____

2. _____

3. _____

After wrapping up this Racial Healing Practice, how do you feel about your next steps in consciousness-raising? As you checked off the resources you would like to benefit from, did you see a preference for the options under "education" or "people"? Did you notice that some of these resources you already turn to in order to raise your race-consciousness? Last question: did you realize that this workbook is one of those resources (wink!)?

Now that you have reflected on some potential sources of race consciousness-raising, let's take it another step further. That step further is taking on a new identity—becoming an "antiracist."

WHAT DOES IT MEAN TO BE ANTIRACIST?

The term "antiracist" refers to people who are actively seeking not only to raise their consciousness about race and racism, but also to take action when they see racial power inequities in everyday life. Being an antiracist is much different from just being "nonracist," as Black antiracist Marlon James (2016) made clear. Being a nonracist means you can have beliefs against racism, but when it comes to events like the murders of Black men by police, "you can watch things at home unfolding on TV, but not do a thing about it." According to James, being an antiracist means that you are developing a different moral code, one that pairs a commitment to not being racist (whether verbalized or not) with action to protest and end the racist things you see in the world. I would add that saying you aren't a racist isn't enough to start healing from racism. You need the intentional mindset of *Yep, this racism thing is everyone's problem—including mine, and I'm going to do something about it.*

Of course, being an antiracist is a different proposition for a person of color than it is for a White person. Let's examine what an antiracist identity looks like on both sides of this binary.

Becoming an Antiracist as a White Person

For White people, becoming an antiracist is a journey that evolves alongside your White racial identity. For instance, once you have moved out of obliviousness about your White privilege, you can move toward integrative awareness of what it means to be White and how to use your White privilege. The stages of using your White privilege to change your internalized racism and to interrupt racism when you see it are a big part of developing an antiracist identity. In her article "White Supremacy Culture: Changework," Tema Okun (2006, 13) talked about antiracism based on her own journey as a White person taking on this identity. I slightly adapted her list of ways to be a White antiracist:

- See yourself as part of the White group.

- Understand and begin to take responsibility for your power and privilege as part of the white group—such as acknowledging the historical roots of White Supremacy and knowing that the White privilege you have as a result of that history is a real thing.

- Have all the feelings related to deepening relationships and increased multicultural experience—both the feelings of guilt, anger, or frustration that can sometimes arise in a racist system in which you experience privilege and the feelings of joy and connection to others that will emerge from pursuing diverse relationships and acting to protest and combat racism you encounter.

- Distinguish between your commitment to being a White antiracist and the part of you that wants to be a *perfect* antiracist—socialization is real, and racism is real, and you won't always be perfectly antiracist.

- Know there will be hard things that come up when you explore White privilege. Learn to see these challenges as "teachers" and opportunities to learn more about your own Whiteness. Instead of getting defensive when these challenges arise, lean into curiosity and cultivate desire for understanding and growth.

- Participate in individual and collective action against racism.

- Value self-reflection on your White identity.

- Use racist thoughts and behaviors you might engage in to deepen understanding and continue to change thoughts and behaviors.

Okun believes that White folks can take on six specific responsibilities to become antiracist in an ongoing process. Being an antiracist is not a one-time event or decision, or an identity you ever finally and fully achieve, but a commitment. Her six responsibilities will remind you of our earlier discussion of raising your race-consciousness through education and people resources. Below are Okun (2006)'s six Rs:

1. **Read** and educate yourself on the effects, impacts, and other structures of racism.

2. **Reflect** on what this education means for you as someone developing a White antiracist identity, such as identifying new ways to challenge everyday racism and work on racial justice initiatives.

3. **Remember** how you participate in the thoughts, beliefs, and actions that uphold racism, whether you intend to or not, and how you "forget" that racism exists. Identify internalized racial attitudes you have about people of color.

4. Take **risks** to challenge racism when you see it or realize when you are participating in it. Interrupt racial stereotypes when you hear them, and support people of color in your personal and professional settings when they speak out about their experiences with racism.

5. **Rejection** is something you'll experience as an antiracist, as sometimes you will make mistakes and "get it wrong" when it comes to identifying and challenging racism. Because of your White privilege, it will sometimes be tough to identify how something you are doing may be harmful to people of color. And people of color may reject what you are saying and even more so hold you accountable for these missteps. Learn to understand and accept rejection. People of color have justified anger about racism, and they may reject you or White people harshly because of it. If this happens, understand that this is the product of their treatment at the hands of a racist system. Don't take it personally; rather, help them if you can and continue to stay in the fight against racism.

6. **Relationship building** is a part of what you do along the way—with White folks and people of color who are somewhere on their journey from nonracist to antiracist.

Let's look at an example of what becoming a White antiracist using these six Rs looks like in the real world. Michael, a White, twenty-year-old college student, grew up in a homogenously White family and neighborhood and attended predominantly White schools. He moved to a racially diverse area for the first time when he went to college and had a roommate who was a person of color. Michael realized that people around him had experiences he didn't know much about, and that he himself could be behaving in ways that disrespected people of color in ways he might not even be realizing. Michael decided to take a college course on diversity in his first year and began working on learning more about his White privilege and how to become an antiracist. We can look at the steps he took in terms of Okun's six Rs:

1. Michael **read** and educated himself on what White privilege was. He considered the effects it had on his own life in terms of lost opportunities to interact with people of color and learn a more truthful history of the world as it related to race and racism, and what it meant for people of color to lack such privilege. As he read and educated himself, he learned about the impacts of racism on other racial groups and how structures of racism are upheld in current times.

2. Michael began to **reflect** on what this education meant for him. He wanted to cast aside the obliviousness he had about racism and White privilege. He knew that being an antiracist would mean identifying ways he had previously ignored everyday racism that people of color experienced (e.g., he remembered the one Latinx student in his middle school class being called racial epithets and not realizing how these were racist acts) and racial microaggressions he had enacted (e.g., assuming Asian Americans were recent immigrants). He joined an antiracist campus group, where he and other folks with White privilege could interrupt everyday racism and work on larger campus racial justice initiatives.

3. Michael made sure to **remember** throughout his antiracist work that he would inevitably "forget" about racism and its systems because that is how racism works. He kept educating himself on the different ways White privilege can show up (e.g., feeling guilty about racism, not having to think about race, not being extraordinarily worried when pulled over by police for a traffic ticket, not knowing the history of the land his campus was on and who the indigenous peoples were). He also intentionally explored negative racial stereotypes he still held about people of color and sought to expand the diversity of people in his life.

4. Michael took **risks** to challenge racism when he saw it in his classes, like when his professors wouldn't call on his fellow students of color. He also assumed a leadership role in his residence hall, and he challenged his fellow White student leaders to think about how their racial privilege influenced selection of programming for their dorm.

5. Michel knew to expect **rejection** from people of color when he made a racist assumption or was misusing his White privilege. For instance, sometimes he was so excited about his efforts to be an antiracist, he would talk over people of color doing similar work and minimize their contributions. He learned to apologize as soon as he noticed this was happening or when a person of color brought this to his attention. He learned not only to welcome the feedback

he would get from people of color when he had a misstep, but also to value this feedback as a way to grow as a White antiracist.

6. **Relationship building** was the major focus of what Michael did throughout each of the previous steps. He learned to make connections with White folks who wanted to externalize their racially stereotyped notions of the world and to build relationships with people of color. Through relationship building, Michael eventually had a vibrant, diverse group of people in his life who could not only support and inspire him in his antiracist identity development, but also hold him accountable for his missteps and growth.

You can see that becoming an antiracist is an ongoing practice and process, exactly opposite of color blindness. You want to be able to see and identify everything about racism. You want to know what your part in racism is. You continuously raise your race-consciousness. And you do this alongside a multitude of different types of people on the same journey. You expect the feelings of anger, frustration, sadness, rage, irritation, grief, and other emotions as you challenge racism, as we discussed in chapter 4.

Becoming an Antiracist as a Person of Color

People of color can also claim an antiracist identity, with all that this entails: consciousness of race and racism as it manifests in the world, and a commitment to speak out and act against racism they encounter in the world. Remember, for people of color, that first stage of racial identity development is often obliviousness about racism existing, which lasts until that first critical incident of being the target of a racist act or idea. Once people of color become aware of racism, however, they become capable of having negative ideas about the races of other people of color. This is exactly the kind of behavior that claiming and living an antiracist life can help you challenge. For example, there are plenty of opportunities for me to apply Okun's antiracist steps with people in my Indian American and South Asian community who hold negative racial attitudes about other people of color groups.

Why does this within-group racism exist? Well, the roots are in how colonization has been internalized. British colonization of South Asian lands made it imperative that people in those lands adopt the values and ways of life that the British set for them in order to survive. This left many brown folks with the internalized notion that White culture and White values were the civilized and highly regarded ones to emulate—and that people who are deemed aberrant by White colonizers' values, like Black people, are to be denigrated. You may have also noticed that Black folks may have negative ideas about Asian Americans, and vice versa. Well, people of Asian heritage enter a US racial context where Black people were enslaved, denigrated, and seen as inferior. Black people learn—like most US citizens—very little about people of Asian heritage, except that they represent something that is foreign and a threat (as discussed in chapter 3). This is especially true of Asian Americans who don't speak English and maintain traditions from their home cultures. It can be so frustrating—and infuriating—to see people of color groups tear one another down!

Developing an antiracist identity as people of color means recognizing that all racial groups are struggling in some way under White supremacy. It means recognizing that people of color groups are not always united in solidarity under a larger umbrella of people of color. Misinformation, prejudice, and harm can exist between people of color groups, and these need to be confronted just as White racism must be challenged. This means knowing how different enslavement and immigration histories you learned about in chapter 3 influence the different histories of oppression each racial group has. This also means recognizing there are important class differences that can have a big impact on the degree of oppression people of color experience (class privilege can buffer experiences of racism, as you will explore in chapter 8).

You can take action and challenge internalized White supremacy by interrupting the patterns in which people of color of one racial group hold prejudices against another racial group. You can speak up when someone in your family or work setting expresses such a sentiment (see chapter 7 for more on doing this). By doing things like this on an individual and systemic level, you can create solidarity with other racial groups while acknowledging the important differences in how racism is meted out across racial groups. Further, in doing so, you can create the possibility of collective action against racism on multiple individual and systemic levels. For example, you can talk with people across racial groups and collectively identify the differences and similarities racism has on all racial groups. Then, people of color can focus more effectively on challenging White supremacy as a larger collective (more on this in chapter 10).

For people of color, Okun's (2006) list of antiracist principles still applies. But I would tweak it a bit to ensure that you as a person of color are examining the specific biases you have internalized about other racial groups and your own, as I've described below:

1. **Read** and educate yourself on the effects, impacts, and other structures of racism—both on your racial group and on other groups.

2. **Reflect** on what this education means for you as someone developing an antiracist identity.

3. **Remember** how you might be participating in thoughts, beliefs, and actions that uphold racism. Identify the negative beliefs you have internalized about your own race and even apply to other people of color. Think about how you are complicit with racism when racist events are happening—ways you don't speak up for yourself and others.

4. Take **risks** to challenge racism when you see it or realize when you are participating in it.

5. Understand the anger that you and people of other racial groups may have about racism, express your **rejection** of racism from White people, and continue to stay in the fight against racism with a clear understanding of what privileges or disadvantages you may have relative to people of other racial groups. It's okay to be angry about racism—it has hurt you and lots of other people you care about. Turn the anger you have into energy to challenge racism and hold White people accountable for their own racism. (To be clear, in general it isn't your job to hold White folks accountable, but it is an important aspect of being an antiracist person of color.) Keep in mind you have internalized White supremacist notions about your own race and others, so keep a lookout for how those internalized attitudes show up and provide an obstacle to your joining forces with other people of color groups.

6. Engage in **relationship building** with people of color and White folks alike who are on their journey from nonracist to antiracist.

Here's an example of what the six Rs look like for a person of color seeking to be an antiracist. Jasmine is a thirty-three-year-old Native American who recently moved to the west coast from North Dakota to work in a technology start-up company. After the 2016 presidential election, she got more involved in antiracism work. She was particularly moved by the water protectors at Standing Rock protesting against the construction of the Keystone pipeline, and wanted to learn about racial justice.

Let's look at Jasmine's six Rs:

1. Jasmine began to **read** and educate herself on how White supremacy influenced her own Native American tribe and other people of color. She knew about the Black Lives Matter movement, but she had not learned much in her schools about Black history. Jasmine began to read books about the enslavement of Black people and Jim Crow laws. As she read these histories, Jasmine drew parallels between the racism experiences of Black and Native American communities (e.g., stolen land and property, erasure of indigenous cultures and spiritualities). She also read about Black leaders in the civil rights movement, who reminded her of elders in her own tribe who advocated for better resources for her community.

2. Jasmine began to **reflect** on what her (re)education meant for her as a person of color developing an antiracist identity. She paid attention to the different emotions that came up as she read about her tribe and about the experiences of Black people under racism, and she began to talk to other people in her tribe who wanted to learn how to more effectively challenge racism when they noticed it.

3. Jasmine sought to **remember** how her internalized negative beliefs about herself as a Native American and person of color influenced how she felt about herself. She noticed she wouldn't speak up much at work when she had an idea, and she also noticed that other people of color had difficulty being heard when they did speak. She began to notice the opportunities where she could challenge these instances of racism at her workplace.

4. Eventually, Jasmine also took **risks** to interrupt racism at work, and she began to notice racism in everyday life more and more. She noticed that when women of color at her work spoke up, White leaders would often subtly discount their ideas. Jasmine also noticed how sports teams in her city used Native American symbols as mascots. She talked with people she trusted about what she could do in these situations to fight against racism.

5. Jasmine worked with several community groups doing antiracist work, and sometimes she would express her rejection of the ideas White people had about how to do the work. They had good ideas, but sometimes the way they expressed what the group's goals should be didn't seem to center the experiences of non-White people as it should have. She expressed herself and felt better just knowing she said something important that she felt.

6. She also began **relationship building** beyond her tribe, intentionally seeking to connect with people of color and White people who were doing antiracist work. In these relation-ships, she could ask questions about how to confront subtle racism and she could join in initiatives to challenge systemic racism.

By taking the steps above, you learn to recognize more subtle forms of racism, like whose ideas are valued in a meeting and whose are not. You start to realize that many historical landmarks and buildings are named for White people, and rarely for people of color. You notice that you don't see overt racism often, but that the majority of physicians, lawyers, and educators you know are White. And you learn in each of these situations to connect your realizations to some type of action—from educating yourself and others to advocacy and interruption. This continual work is exhausting. If you don't take care of yourself as you do it—stepping back from the flow of your antiracist work from time to time for sleep, water, a healthy meal, friend time, alone time, vacation—it will be difficult to sustain your consciousness-raising efforts. I'll refer back to Marlon James (2016) and say that this does not mean reverting to being a nonracist and doing nothing. Now that you've seen what the six Rs would look like for White and people of color antiracists, I would add a seventh "R" to Okun's list: "(Rest)ore." (Rest)ore means that you understand that being an antiracist requires sustainability, so you find ways to rest when you need to, restore your energy, and nourish yourself in reflection before diving into the work again. See the next Racial Healing Practice to explore where you are in your own antiracist development.

RACIAL HEALING PRACTICE
Becoming an Antiracist

Explore how Okun's six components, plus the seventh step I added—(rest)ore—might fit together to help you develop a more realized antiracist identity. Write about where you think you are for each component—what your strengths might be and where you might need to grow.

1. Read and educate yourself on the effects, impacts, and other structures of racism.

    My strengths: _____

    _____

    _____

    Areas needing growth: _____

    _____

    _____

2. Reflect on what this education means for you as someone developing an antiracist identity.

    My strengths: _____

    _____

    _____

    Areas needing growth: _____

    _____

    _____

3. Remember how you participate in the thoughts, beliefs, and actions that internalize and uphold racism.

    My strengths: _____

    _____

    _____

    Areas needing growth: _____

    _____

    _____

4. Take risks to challenge racism when you see it or realize when you are participating in it.

    My strengths: _____

    _____

    _____

    Areas needing growth: _____

    _____

    _____

5. Rejection is a part of being an antiracist. If you are White and are rejected, hearing the anger that people of color have about racism, you don't take it personally; you allow people of color to have and express that anger. If you are a person of color, you are comfortable with your anger, which helps establish and strengthen the boundaries you have against racism. In both racial groups, you continue to stay in the fight against racism.

    My strengths: _____

    _____

    _____

Areas needing growth: _____

_____

_____

6. Relationship building is a part of what you do along the way—with White folks and people of color who are somewhere on their journey from nonracist to antiracist.

    My strengths: _____

    _____

    _____

    Areas needing growth: _____

    _____

    _____

7. (Rest)ore for the next steps in your antiracist identity.

    My strengths: _____

    _____

    _____

    Areas needing growth: _____

    _____

    _____

What did you learn about yourself in the seven steps? Are there some components you want to refine more right now? Are there people in your life who exhibit some of the components that you would like to grow in whom you can talk with about being an antiracist?

APPLYING RACE-CONSCIOUSNESS TO YOUR EVERYDAY LIFE

Gordon Hodson, who researches prejudice, suggests that it may be rare for people to just flat out say prejudicial things in our society because doing so now has some stigma attached to it (Hodson, Dovodio, and Gaertner 2002). For instance, how often at work will you hear someone call someone else a racial epithet? I am not saying it doesn't happen at all, but it is less commonplace now than it was in the past. More so today, people like to think of themselves as nonracist or color blind, so racism is more covert and tough to identify. However, Hodson and colleagues note that when a more subtle racial prejudice is expressed, people may not say anything that counters it. Why? He says the desire we as humans tend to have for "easy" interactions with one another, where we don't rock the boat, can mean that we become *passive bystanders* when we do see prejudicial ideas and acts. Maybe someone makes a racist joke at the dinner table, and you don't say anything. When you are silent like this, the person assumes you are okay with what they said.

On the other hand, as we just talked about, a big part of developing an antiracist mindset means raising our race-consciousness—and working with others to do so as well. This means we move from being bystanders (where we may notice racism, but don't do anything) to becoming *proactive upstand-ers*. As proactive upstanders, we no longer wait on the sidelines and say and do nothing. We take risks and enter conversational and action spaces where we don't allow racist ideas and acts to just happen without interruption. That means we take some risks in all of our settings—with our family and friends as well as in our relationships at school, work, and other settings.

And when you take those risks, you will experience rejection. If you are White and are interrupting your cousin's racist rant on immigration, you could be called a variety of names or greeted with silence. If you are a person of color and are interrupting internalized racism from your mom (e.g., "I would never go to a Latino physician—they aren't well trained"), you may feel like you are being disrespectful to her by saying something. And then—no matter whether you are White or a person of color—you may get accused of playing the infamous "race card," being a "whiny liberal," or being "politically correct."

As an antiracist, be prepared for some of these responses—not to change another person's mind (you may not be able to do that), but rather to move out of silence and complicity with their enacted or internalized racism. This means raising your race-consciousness in a different way. As you interrupt these prejudices, sharing that you are not in agreement with them, you will hear some of the stereotyped responses. Keep in mind that those stereotyped responses, like "playing the race card," are designed to stop conversations about racism. Not only are they untrue, but also their specific reason ("you are just being politically correct") is to move you into inaction and invalidate what you have to say. The good news is you can use these opportunities to shift the focus in these interactions from minimization and denial of racism to curiosity (remember that healing strategy you worked on in chapter 2?) to open the *potential* opportunity for different conversations. I say "potential" because the strategies we talk about next aren't designed to change someone's belief systems, but rather to show that you are not in agreement with the racist ideas or acts being expressed. Sometimes, this can spur the other person to begin the work of learning about how racism works and raising their race consciousness.

This learning can involve a lot of pain. It can be really painful for White folks to realize they have been participating in White supremacy in ways they did not realize and ways they were ignoring or avoiding, because they see themselves as good people who would never want to hurt anyone. They don't see themselves as hateful people. On the other hand, you might respond, there are lots of White folks who do ascribe to overt racist and hateful views. I think this group of people also experiences pain—but in a different way. If the haters make another racial group the "problem" in society, then they don't have to look at their own inability to find solutions in various situations, in addition to their own fear and pain they would experience in acknowledging there are victims of racism who have suffered from it. As James Baldwin (1955) said, "I imagine one of the reasons people cling to their hates so stubbornly is because they sense, once hate is gone, they will be forced to deal with pain." That pain is why some folks who express racism will use tools of denial and minimization to say, "Nope, racism just isn't real."

So what are the tools that you can use to show you are a proactive upstander when it comes to racism? There are many levels of racial prejudice people can express, so you need to have a few prepared ways of responding for a variety of situations. For instance, you may be responding to something that is subtly racist (e.g., "Why do all the Asian Americans hang out together all the time?"). I often encounter this at work, where people will say things embedded with racism and aren't aware and/or educated about a particular issue. It's not going to help them (or me) if I go on into full "You shouldn't say that ever" mode because they will likely become defensive and shut down about the issue. But I for sure want to challenge their racism, so in more subtle situations, I use curiosity to invite the person into a conversation to say more about what they mean and unpack what they are saying. Typically as they speak more, they actually are able to identify their own racism in what they are saying—or I am able to give them additional education and provide an alternate, more factual, nonracist perspective. On the other hand, you may hear someone say something that is overtly racist ("Native Americans have been getting government handouts for years"). This is something that happens to me a lot in family circles (holiday gatherings!) and in public settings—for instance, the time when I was innocently pumping gas and the person next to me made a racial epithet about a Latinx person. In these overtly racist situations, I need prepared responses that help me let the other person know I'm not okay with what they said and set a boundary with them.

Preparation is the key ingredient in both of these situations. Below are some strategies and sentence stems that that you can use in a range of situations when you hear subtle or overt racism:

- Express curiosity: "Tell me more about _____."

- Offer an alternate perspective: "Have you ever considered _____?"

- Share your disagreement: "I don't see it the way you do. I see it as _____."

- Seek an area of agreement: "We don't agree on _____, but can we agree on _____?"

- Ask to continue the conversation at a later time: "Could we revisit this conversation about _____ tomorrow?"

- Set a boundary: "Please do not say _____ again to me or around me."

These are just a few examples of how you can develop race-aware responses in your interactions with others. I can't emphasize enough how helpful it is to practice using these responses. When you practice, you notice the feelings that come up in you, the ways you want to shut down or shut the other person down, and lots of other less-than-helpful patterns.

Do the next Racial Healing Practice to explore how these ideas apply to your own life and to get some of that practice.

RACIAL HEALING PRACTICE
Becoming an Antiracist in the "Real World"

Think of a time you heard someone in your life—in your family or at work or school—say something racist or that reflected internalized racism. Once you have that incident in mind, write your response to the following:

Did you respond to this person? Why or why not?

_____

_____

_____

_____

_____

_____

_____

What emotions came up for you during this event? What did you notice about your body? Did your body tense up or freeze? Did you feel tightness or some other sensation in your back, shoulders, pit of your belly, or somewhere else?

_____

_____

_____

_____

_____

_____

_____

Did you share your feelings with the person? What would you say to this person if you did share your feelings?

_____

_____

_____

_____

_____

Next, apply a few of the following sentence stems to what you might have said to this person in this interaction to practice a bit.

Express curiosity: Tell me more about _____

_____

_____.

Offer an alternate perspective: Have you ever considered _____

_____

_____.

Share your disagreement: I don't see it the way you do. I see it as _____

_____

_____.

Seek an area of agreement: We don't agree on _____,

but can we agree on _____

_____?

Ask to continue the conversation at a later time: Could we revisit this conversation about _____ tomorrow?

Set a boundary: Please do not say _____
again to me or around me.

How did your practice go? Notice any areas to improve on right away? Are there people in your life with whom you can practice for the next time you are in a similar situation? We will talk more about these interruption skills in chapter 9 (Be a Racial Ally), but for now know that developing proactive interruption skills when it comes to racism are part of raising your race-consciousness.

RACIAL HEALING WRAP-UP

Raising your race-consciousness means seeking out the resources you need when it comes to education and people to help you better understand how your own race and racism works in the world. Joseph Campbell (1988, 155) may have talked about consciousness-raising the best: "When we quit thinking primarily about ourselves and our own self-preservation, we undergo a truly heroic transformation of consciousness." When you raise your own race-consciousness in a consistent and ongoing way, you have the opportunity to develop an antiracist identity that puts you in a collective of other antiracist White folks and folks of color taking similar action. You move from being a passive bystander in racism to taking a proactive upstander and interrupter stance. That means you interact with people in your everyday life pretty differently because you are continuously seeking to raise your own race-consciousness. This leads us into the next chapter, where you'll learn the racial healing strategy of catching yourself in the flow of racism.

CHAPTER 6

Catch Yourself in the Flow of Racism

Because racism is pretty much everywhere, you will find yourself in racialized situations in school, work, family, and social settings. As much as you strive to raise your racial consciousness as a White person or person of color, as you explored in chapter 5, you will unexpectedly find yourself in what I like to call the "flow of racism." You could be going through your everyday life getting coffee, meeting a friend for lunch, or attending a family function—and all of a sudden you witness racism (overt or convert) or notice internalized racism in yourself or others.

You thought you were just getting coffee, but you were really confronted with an opportunity to interact or act differently in these racialized situations. We all know how terrible it feels to hear a racist joke and not know what to say. And then there are the more subtle forms of racism that can be just as challenging to know how to handle, like a White person saying, "I am not racist; I have friends who are people of color," or a person of color displaying internalized racism, saying, "I don't think I would go to a doctor who is a person of color." In this chapter, you'll learn to identify when racism is happening and how to interrupt the flow of racism.

NOTICING WHEN RACIAL MICROAGGRESSIONS HAPPEN

Harvard University psychiatrist and professor Chester Pierce (1970) used the term "microaggressions" to describe the everyday, automatic, and negative racialized messages that people of color receive because of their racial group. Derald Wing Sue (2010), psychologist and researcher at Columbia University, expanded Pierce's work, defining microaggressions as the brief, daily indignities that people of color experience when these negative, everyday messages are conveyed to them—for instance, when they're stereotyped (e.g., a Black man being told, "You speak so articulately"), exoticized (e.g., a Japanese American woman being told, "You look just like a China doll," or a Native American two-spirit person being told, "Can you do a powwow?"), or pathologized (a Black woman being told, "I just don't understand why Black women are always so angry"). Sue and colleagues (2007) distinguish three types of racial microaggressions:

- *Microassaults*—intentional acts of racism designed to harm a person of color (e.g., a wait staff giving preferential treatment to a White person over a person of color, using racist language)

- *Microinsults*—possibly unintentional acts of racism that deliver a hidden message insulting to a person of color (e.g., statements that imply people of color received a job or promotion based on their skin color)

- *Microinvalidations*—messages that diminish the lived realities of people of color (e.g., being asked, "Why do you always have to make things about race?" or being told, "I don't see race. I'm color blind.")

One racial microaggression I hear repeatedly from well-meaning White folks about my mixed-race identity is "I can't tell what you are." When I first encountered this microaggression, it hurt. It reinforced a message that I didn't fit, and that the racial ambiguity of my skin color was a problem that people who met me urgently needed to solve. This microaggression also hurt because I had experienced not fitting in both Indian and White groups, so it just drove that message in more deeply. Part of the hurt and pain had to do with the dialogue in my head. I tried to ascribe a rationale for why it happened, saying things like:

- *Did that really happen?*

- *They didn't mean any harm in saying that.*

- *They're just curious, I guess.*

- *Well, they are right, I don't really fit a racial group.*

- *Well, what am I really?*

And these are just snippets of some of the questions and dialogue that would go on in my mind afterward. You could argue that questions like "What are you?" reflect the human need to understand others, which is the product of one's own socialization in which our own race and the race of others is assumed to really matter. But because racism is persistent and systemic, we have to acknowledge this human drive to understand others is not neutral. Racism divides people up into those who are assumed "normal" and those assumed to be the "other."

Another reason for the hurt and pain I experienced was the repeated nature of microaggressions. Weighing these questions and dealing with my own thoughts about my racial identity as a result of the microaggression took time and energy. I felt mentally exhausted afterward. Even though I had heard the question a lot, the fact was I was not prepared. My family didn't prepare me for this question. My school didn't prepare me for this question. And I didn't prepare me for this question. So I was caught off guard. Every. Single. Time. It took me a minute to realize that part of my racial healing was to prepare for the question, so I wasn't so drained and shocked each time it happened. Now, I know these types of questions are microaggressions so I can interrupt them quicker than ever, which allows me to then make sure I am not internalizing negative ideas about my racial identity. I can also interrupt this type of microaggression with a verbal response that sets a clear boundary ("It's not okay to ask me 'what' I am like I am an object"), humor ("Funny you would ask me that—actually, why would you ask me that?"), or even curiosity ("That's such an interesting question—why would you ask me that?"). Each of these interruptions helps me to preserve my energy and as a result protect my mental health. I learned that I could interrupt the flow of racism—and it definitely took practice.

Sue and colleagues (2007) described nine themes common to microaggressions that send specific negative messages to people of color, as shown in the table below.

Examples of Racial Microaggressions

Themes	Microaggression	Message
Alien in own land When Asian Americans and Latinx Americans are assumed to be foreign-born	"Where are you from?" "Where were you born?" "You speak good English."	You are not American.
	A person asking an Asian American to teach them words in their native language	You are a foreigner.

Themes	Microaggression	Message
Ascriptions of intelligence Assigning intelligence to a person of color on the basis of their race	"You are a credit to your race." "You are so articulate." Asking an Asian person to help with a math or science problem	People of color are generally not as intelligent as Whites. It is unusual for someone of your race to be intelligent. All Asians are intelligent and good in math/sciences.
Color blindness Statements that indicate a White person does not want to acknowledge race	"When I look at you, I don't see color." "America is a melting pot." "There is only one race, the human race."	I am denying your racial/ethnic experiences as a person of color. Assimilate/acculturate to dominant culture. I am denying you as a racial/cultural being.
Criminality/assumptions of criminal status A person of color is presumed to be dangerous, criminal, or deviant on the basis of their race	A White man or woman clutching their purse or checking their wallet as a Black person approaches or passes A store owner following a customer of color around the store A White person waits to ride the next elevator when a person of color is on it.	You are a criminal. You are going to steal. You are poor/You do not belong. You are dangerous.
Denial of individual racism A statement made when Whites deny their racial biases	"I'm not a racist. I have several Black friends." "As a woman, I know what you go through as a racial minority."	I am immune to racism because I have friends of color. Your racial oppression is no different than my gender oppression. I can't be a racist. I'm like you.

Themes	Microaggression	Message
Myth of meritocracy Statements which assert that race does not play a role in life successes	"I believe the most qualified person should get the job." "Everyone can succeed in this society if they work hard enough."	People of color are given extra unfair benefits because of their race. People of color are lazy and/or incompetent and need to work harder.
Pathologizing cultural values/communication styles The notion that the values and communication styles of the dominant/White culture are ideal.	Asking a Black person: "Why do you have to be so loud/ animated? Just calm down." To an Asian or Latinx person: "Why are you so quiet? We want to know what you think. Be more verbal." "Speak up more." Dismissing an individual who brings up race/culture in a work/school setting	Assimilate to dominant culture. Leave your cultural baggage outside.
Second-class citizen Occurs when a White person is given preferential treatment as a consumer over a person of color	Person of color mistaken for a service worker Having a taxi cab pass a person of color and pick up a White passenger Being ignored at a store counter as attention is given to the White customer behind you "You people…"	People of color are servants to Whites. They couldn't possibly occupy high-status positions. You are likely to cause trouble and/or travel to a dangerous neighborhood. Whites are more valued customers than people of color. You don't belong. You are a lesser being.

Themes	Microaggression	Message
Environmental microaggressions Macro-level microaggressions, which are more apparent on systemic and environmental levels	A college or university with buildings that are all named after White heterosexual upper class males Television shows and movies that feature predominantly White people, without representation of people of color Overcrowding of public schools in communities of color Overabundance of liquor stores in communities of color	You don't belong/You won't succeed here. There is only so far you can go. You are an outsider/You don't exist. People of color don't/ shouldn't value education. People of color are deviant.

(Sue et al. 2007; reprinted with permission)

Now it's time to dig a little deeper into microaggressions. If you're White, you'll explore the ones that you have enacted yourself. If you're a person of color, you'll have an opportunity to write about the racial microaggressions you have experienced from others. Because people of color can also commit racial microaggressions toward specific groups (e.g., a South Asian American who assumes a Latinx person was born in Mexico), if you're a person of color you can reflect on those you might have unintentionally enacted. As you dive into this next Racial Healing Practice, be as honest with yourself as you can about your experiences.

RACIAL HEALING PRACTICE
Exploring Personal Experiences of Racial Microaggressions

Racial microaggressions have very personal effects. For people of color, they can stimulate feelings of self-doubt and internalized racism. For White people, committing a microaggression is harmful to people of color, and it ultimately serves as a barrier in your relationship with them because of the distrust it creates. So it's important to take an honest look at microaggressions you commit and/or experience. Respond to the following questions to explore more of your personal experiences of racial microaggressions.

Think back to a time when you heard or committed a racial microaggression—something that would qualify as an indignity for a person of color. Write it here, and then identify the theme and embedded message.

_____

_____

_____

_____

Racial microaggression theme: _____

Racial microaggression message: _____

What were your thoughts, feelings, and behaviors *during* this racial microaggression—in the moments you were experiencing it?

What I thought: _____

_____

What I felt: _____

_____

What I did: _____

_____

For White readers: What motivated you to act as you did?

_____

_____

_____

_____

_____

_____

What were your thoughts, feelings, and behaviors *after* this racial microaggression?

What I thought: _____

_____

What I felt: _____

_____

What I did: _____

_____

For readers of color: What were the effects of the experience? What message did it convey to you about yourself or other people? How long did it continue to affect your emotions and experiences?

_____

_____

_____

_____

_____

_____

_____

Now that you have explored a personal experience of committing a racial microaggression (as a White person) or experiencing a racial microaggression (as a person of color), take a moment to explore which of Sue and colleagues' (2007) nine racial microaggression categories you commit or experience most frequently. Rank the list below from 1 (most frequent) to 9 (least frequent).

_____   Alien in own land

_____   Ascriptions of intelligence

_____   Color blindness

_____   Criminality/assumptions of criminal status

_____   Denial of individual racism

_____   Myth of meritocracy

_____   Pathologizing cultural values/communication styles

_____   Second-class citizen

_____   Environmental microaggressions

What did you notice about your rankings of racial microaggressions? As you look at the most frequent ones you experience (as a person of color) or commit (as a White person), what are the feelings associated with the ones that are most frequent or least frequent? Are feelings of shame, guilt, self-doubt, anger, fear, sadness, or other emotions associated more or less with some of the categories on the list?

Now, how do you respond to a microaggression you experience or inadvertently commit?

The best way for a person of color to minimize the harm of experiencing racial microaggressions is to notice what's happening as soon as possible and be able to interrupt and respond by setting a boundary. You can do this through your internal dialogue (*That is this person's problem and doesn't reflect on me* or *Ouch, that hurt; I need to connect with someone who can support me*) or external dialogue ("You can't say that to me" or "That's not an okay thing to say"). You do need to acknowledge and validate the feelings that come up for you, too. If you experience anger, you may need to breathe through that anger before you channel it into setting a boundary. If you experience fear, you may need to take care of yourself and digest what has happened before you set a boundary. As a White person, the prescriptions are the same: learn to notice when microaggressions are happening and how to act quickly in response. It's good for White people to practice noticing a racial microaggression more immediately, especially if you have committed it, so you can apologize, do any needed repair work in your relationship, and do your internal work to interrogate why it happened.

When I talk about responses to microaggressions, I use the categories of internal and external dialogue for a few reasons. Sometimes racial microaggressions are happening within a context that is pretty unsafe—like in a predominantly White environment, or while you are traveling outside of your home, or even during a job evaluation for promotion—in which you could face repercussions for speaking out. So it might not always be safe, as a person of color, to externalize your thoughts to the person committing the microaggression. But it is always important to be on top of your game with your internal dialogue, so you can lessen the chances that you internalize the negative embedded message in the racial microaggression.

As a White person, safety is also relative, but you likely have more power and privilege to respond to a racial microaggression if you witness it. Going back to the personal example I shared earlier, I remember one day at work, a White woman referring to my race asked me, "I just can't figure out what you are—I mean what are you?" My White friend at work interjected and said, "Hey, that's a messed up question to ask—do you want to hear 'What are you?' like you are an object?"

Was it a risk for my White friend to say this as her colleague? Sure. Maybe her colleague would've had negative feelings toward her afterward, or maybe this colleague might have become her supervisor at a later time. But she used her White privilege anyway, because in her internal dialogue with herself as a White woman, she was able to notice the racial microaggression right away and say, *This is a racial microaggression, and I am going to say something because this is not okay.* Her internal dialogue led her to have an external dialogue that actively interrupted and redirected what was happening. An important thing to keep in mind is that my friend didn't act out of expectation of a reward or to get a "thank you." She acted because she knew what was right, and she was prepared and able to interrupt the racial microaggression. As a person of color, I must say it was a relief to not have to respond in the moment. And my internal dialogue reminded me that I knew exactly who I was as a mixed-race person and that I am not some confused racial being or object.

In the next Racial Healing Practice, you'll look more closely at your own experiences with racial microaggressions.

RACIAL HEALING PRACTICE
Delving Deeper Into Personal
Experiences of Racial Microaggressions

Revisit the top three racial microaggressions on your list in the last Racial Healing Practice, "Exploring Personal Experiences of Racial Microaggressions," and reflect a little more deeply on these experiences. For the racial microaggression you ranked #1 in frequency of committing or experiencing, identify the internal dialogue and external dialogue that can help you respond in a more helpful way.

Your #1 ranked racial microaggression category: _____

What statement in this category do you most often hear?

_____

What is your typical internal dialogue in response to this racial microaggression?

_____

_____

_____

What is your typical external dialogue in response to this racial microaggression?

_____

_____

_____

How could you refine your typical internal dialogue in response to this racial microaggression so you don't further internalize racism (as a person of color) or further commit microaggressions or allow others to commit them with no response (as a White person)?

_____

_____

_____

_____

Your #2 ranked racial microaggression category: _____

What statement in this category do you most often hear?

_____

What is your typical internal dialogue in response to this racial microaggression?

_____

_____

_____

What is your typical external dialogue in response to this racial microaggression?

_____

_____

_____

How could you refine your typical internal dialogue in response to this racial microaggression so you don't further internalize racism (as a person of color) or further commit microaggressions or allow others to commit them with no response (as a White person)?

_____

_____

_____

_____

Your #3 ranked racial microaggression category: _____

What statement in this category do you most often hear?

_____

What is your typical internal dialogue in response to this racial microaggression?

_____

_____

_____

What is your typical external dialogue in response to this racial microaggression?

_____

_____

_____

How could you refine your typical internal dialogue in response to this racial microaggression so you don't further internalize racism (as a person of color) or further commit microaggressions or allow others to commit them with no response (as a White person)?

_____

_____

_____

_____

How did it feel to list your typical internal and external dialogues? What did you learn about yourself as you explored your typical responses to racial microaggressions? When you had an opportunity to practice revising your response internally and externally, did you significantly revise your responses? Do you feel more prepared for the next time you hear these things? I hope so, as the thing about racial microaggressions is that they keep happening. And they keep happening with lots of frequency. Remember that people of any racial group can commit microaggressions—and they are painful to experience and witness. One of the key ways to heal from racism is to increase the capacity in ourselves and others to interrupt how we internalize, commit, and allow racial microaggressions to happen.

NOTICING WHEN RACIAL MACROAGGRESSIONS HAPPEN

Just as you dove more deeply into your experiences involving microaggressions, it's time to dig in more to what racial *macroaggressions* have looked like in your life. Racial macroaggressions are those overt acts of racism that may be enacted individually but definitely reflect the system of racism in that they are persistent, purposeful, and designed to create incapacitating effects for people of color (Osanloo, Boske, and Newcomb 2016). In other words, macroaggressions are instances of prejudice enacted with a purpose: to uphold White supremacy and target people of color. I think of macroaggressions as falling into the following categories:

- *Racial stereotyping and profiling*—attaching racist ideas to a group of people of color and then applying those racist ideas to all individuals from that particular racial group.

- *Racial harassment*—verbal, physical, sexual, and spiritual violence toward people of color that is motivated by the racist idea that people of color are inferior to White people.

Like microaggressions, racial macroaggressions are committed across settings—in public and private, in schools and communities, and in homes and between friends as well as strangers. If you look back in time, racial macroaggressions were pretty easy to see. Lynchings of Black people (physical racial harassment), internment of Japanese US citizens during World War II (racial stereotyping and profiling), stealing of tribal lands from Native Americans (physical racial harassment), and forcing Native American and Mexican American students into Christian-based schools are all examples of racial macroaggressions *mandated* on the systematic level and *enforced* or reinforced on the individual level.

Racial macroaggressions can be overt and violent as well. Race-based hate crimes (at least those that are reported—many are not reported) are increasing, with six out of ten reported hate crimes targeting a person's race (U.S. Department of Justice 2016). You can see how some of the racial macroaggressions can overlap: racial stereotyping and profiling can lead to—and even co-occur with—racial harassment.

On the other hand, racial macroaggressions can be somewhat covert and hard to detect. Recent studies looking at hiring practices show differential treatment for people's resumes that have any form of distinguishable "ethnic" heritage (e.g., a last name of Patel as opposed to Smith; Banerjee, Reitz, and Oreopoulos 2017; Widner and Chicoine 2011). Other employment studies indicate that when people of color "Whiten" their names, their chances of getting hired increase dramatically (Kang et al. 2016), which is why an East Asian person may use a name like Laura on her resume, instead of Zhenqui.

It can be tempting to think racial macroaggressions are a thing of the past. People (even me at an earlier point in my life) can have a "color blind" approach, saying things like "Well, that type of stuff doesn't happen anymore. I was raised to treat everyone the same—I don't see color." However, when you spend time really reflecting on how racism works, you quickly realize that just isn't true.

Often racial macroaggressions can be unchecked and unchallenged, which then suggests acceptance and agreement for the system of racism. For instance, President Trump committed a verbal macroaggression when he called Mexican people attempting to enter the US "animals." Many people condemned those in his party for not speaking out more to challenge this racial macroaggression—as their silence implied consent to his racist words and ideas. Many people did challenge his racial macroaggression. For instance, Clint Smith (2018; author of TED Talks "The Danger of Silence" and "How to Raise a Black Son in America") Tweeted about the danger of the president's use of words in light of the history of racism:

> When the president uses dehumanizing language about entire groups of [people] it can't be understood only as offensive, but as the type of thing that's always preceded enslavement, genocide [and] mass expulsion. To see it *only* as offensive is to misunderstand its potential ramifications. (May 16, 2018, 3:19 p.m.)

Smith's point is clear. Racial macroaggressions are not just offensive—they are like the canary in the coal mine in that they can signal more significant racism to come. Smith chose to challenge this racial macroaggression that was happening on a national level with a Tweet. There are numerous other ways you might respond to a macroaggression that you witness individually or see going on in the national stage. Here are some:

- Engage in an internal dialogue, seeking to challenging the internalized racism that a macroaggression might provoke (whether about your own racial identity or another's).

- Initiate an external dialogue with others about the event and about coalition building in support of the person being harassed or wronged.

- Support someone who's being yelled at or intimidated by a racist person by moving physically closer to them so they're not alone.

- Provide first aid to someone after a physical altercation related to a racist macroaggression.

- Film a racist incident: pull out your phone and record and document the racist macroaggression. It's a strategy people have used with some success to bring attention to racial macroaggressions. Consider your own safety and the safety of the person experiencing the macroaggression if you choose to document it.

- Find relevant local organizations you could donate time or resources to, as a more karmic gesture of restitution in response to incidents in which you're not able or prepared to directly intervene.

Let's check in on your capacity to notice what a racial macroaggression is, when it's happening, what is going on inside of you, and how you can respond in the next Racial Healing Practice.

RACIAL HEALING PRACTICE
Exploring Personal Experiences of
Racial Macroaggressions

Think about the following examples of macroaggressions, write about some of your internal and external dialogue, and then consider what a response might be. Write the first things that come to your mind.

Racial Profiling and Stereotyping

You hear someone at your school, university, or work say, "Mexican families don't really care about education. Their families are usually uneducated."

What would be your typical internal dialogue in response to this racial profiling and stereotyping?

_____

_____

_____

What would be your typical external dialogue in response to this racial profiling and stereotyping?

_____

_____

_____

How could you refine your typical internal dialogue in response to this racial profiling and stereotyping so you don't further internalize racism (as a person of color) or allow others to commit these acts with no response (as a White person)?

_____

_____

_____

_____

Racial Harassment—Verbal Violence

You are at a gas station and go in to pay for your gas. You hear a White person say to the Indian American cashier, "Why do you Indians own all the convenience stores?"

What would be your typical internal dialogue in response to this verbal racial harassment?

_____

_____

_____

What would be your typical external dialogue in response to this verbal racial harassment?

_____

_____

_____

_____

How could you refine your typical internal dialogue in response to this verbal racial harassment so you don't further internalize racism (as a person of color) or allow others to commit these acts with no response (as a White person)?

_____

_____

_____

_____

Racial Harassment—Physical Violence

You see a White person physically push a Latinx person to the ground, yelling, "Go home, illegal."

What would be your typical internal dialogue in response to this physical racial harassment?

_____

_____

_____

What would be your typical external dialogue in response to this physical racial harassment?

_____

_____

_____

_____

How could you refine your typical internal dialogue in response to this physical racial harassment so you don't further internalize racism (as a person of color) or allow others to commit these acts with no response (as a White person)?

_____

_____

_____

_____

Racial Harassment—Sexual Violence

You watch a YouTube video about the history of Native American tribes pre-colonization, which included sexual assault as a colonization tactic. You read the comments, and one said, "Native Americans were too weak to protect their women from rape. They died out anyways."

What would be your typical internal dialogue in response to this sexual racial harassment?

_____

_____

_____

What would be your typical external dialogue in response to this sexual racial harassment?

_____

_____

_____

_____

How could you refine your typical internal dialogue in response to this sexual racial harassment so you don't further internalize racism (as a person of color) or allow others to commit these acts with no response (as a White person)?

_____

_____

_____

_____

Racial Harassment—Spiritual Violence

You are walking down the street, and you hear someone say to a Muslim woman with a hijab, "I don't know why you women put up with men making you cover your hair."

What would be your typical internal dialogue in response to this spiritual racial harassment?

_____

_____

_____

What would be your typical external dialogue in response to this spiritual racial harassment?

_____

_____

_____

_____

How could you refine your typical internal dialogue in response to this spiritual racial harassment so you don't further internalize racism (as a person of color) or allow others to commit these acts with no response (as a White person)?

_____

_____

_____

_____

Did you see some of the overlap between the categories of racial macroaggressions that we talked about earlier? Did the examples remind you of stories you've heard from a friend, family, or community member—or of a national story? Did part of you want to say, "Oh, this would never happen"? Or could you easily see something like this occurring? Or have some of these instances happened to you directly—or been committed by you directly? Did you have an emotional or bodily reaction (that's important to pay attention to) when you were responding? If so, what would you need to do to take care of yourself in that type of situation?

As difficult as it is to delve into these examples, the more you consider that these racial macroaggressions do happen and how, and what you might need to do in response (i.e., stand up for yourself or someone else and take care of yourself in the aftermath), the more you are prepared. And it's the way this knowledge and preparation enables you to think and act differently that helps you and others heal from racism.

RACIAL HEALING WRAP-UP

In this chapter, you got to dive deeply into racial microaggressions and macroaggressions. You learned about the different types that exist and about your typical internal and external dialogue in response. You also began to think about how to shift your own attitudes and beliefs when you are witnessing or committing racial microaggressions and macroaggressions as a White person, or experiencing them as a person of color. Next up, you will learn more about how racism influences your personal and professional relationships.

CHAPTER 7

Understand Racism in Relationships

Chance the Rapper famously said, "The problem is that my [millennial] generation was pacified into believing that racism existed only in our history books" (Welteroth 2017, para 25). He's right—racism is not a past phenomenon, but a real and present one that influences who we develop relationships with throughout our lives. In this chapter, you will learn to map racism's influence in your relationships. You'll explore how racism shapes how you form relationships, including friendships, intimate relationships, and work relationships; how you make decisions about your personal and professional communities; and how your decisions about where to live, work, and play influence it all. Later, in chapter 8, you'll look at the intersectionality of identities (e.g., gender, class) that can also influence race and relationships.

RACE AND FRIENDSHIPS

There's an Irish proverb that goes something like this: "A good friend is like a four-leaf clover, hard to find and lucky to have." You may be nodding your head in agreement. Well, consider the historical context of racism you read about in chapter 3. Not only is a friend who really, really "gets" you tough to find, but it is also even more challenging to develop friendships across racial groups if you grow up in a homogenous neighborhood, school, or other community setting.

If we go back to history again, you can see the broad effects of racial segregation on the development of communities. Native Americans, who were often nomadic groups, were forced onto US-designated "tribal lands" that restricted the land of their communities. African Americans not only experienced slavery, but were also promised "forty acres and a mule," which they never received. In addition, African Americans faced extensive housing discrimination (e.g., because of racist banking practices, African Americans were refused home loans and were therefore unable to purchase homes, instead having to rely on rental housing). This made it challenging, for instance, to move to the suburbs, where schools generally had more economic resources. As immigrants came into the US, many racial groups "stuck together" and benefited from being in the same neighborhoods as people with similar cultural backgrounds and practices. Not a bad thing, right? However, this sticking together furthered the isolation of certain groups and reinforced disparities between them—especially between the lighter-skinned immigrants who "became White" and came to enjoy the privileges associated with that status, and darker-skinned immigrants who were marginalized by White supremacist assumptions and didn't feel safe leaving the neighborhoods that became "theirs."

It's kind of creepy to think that historical events around race influenced the neighborhood you grew up in and live in now, and therefore the friendships you can develop. But, when you start to think about it, it makes total sense. Sure, people develop friendships in places other than their neighborhood, school, or community (e.g., social media, places of worship), but for the most part the decisions you or your family have made, are making, or will make about where to live, work, and play have a powerful influence on the diversity of races within your personal and professional networks. Respond to the next Racial Healing Practice to explore more about this in your life.

RACIAL HEALING PRACTICE
Reflecting on My Friendships over My Lifetime

Friendship is a powerful thing; we can have friends who are like family to us, and friends who are more like acquaintances. Also, your personality can influence your development of friendships. You may have mostly had one friend you were really close to or a lot of friends you were besties with, depending on whether you are an introvert or extrovert. For this practice, respond to each question with the first significant (however you define that) friendship that comes to mind.

Who was your first friend? Was their race different from or similar to yours? How did you come to be friends with them?

_____

_____

_____

_____

_____

_____

Who has been your best friend in your life thus far? Is their race different from or similar to yours? How did you come to be friends with them?

_____

_____

_____

_____

_____

_____

Who has been your closest friend whose race is different from yours? (If this overlaps with the previous questions, select a different friend.) What has it been like to be in an interracial friendship with them?

_____

_____

_____

_____

_____

When you think about your friendships growing up, did your friends mostly share your same race? What was that like?

_____

_____

_____

_____

When you think about your friendships now, do your friends mostly share your same race? What is that like for you?

_____

_____

_____

_____

When you think of the racial patterns you have in friendships throughout your life, what are the top three patterns you would like to shift?

1. _____

2. _____

3. _____

Were your friendship groups mostly people who were different or shared your racial group? What were the reasons for that diversity or lack of diversity in your friendship group? Are there similar racial patterns in your friendships today, or have these patterns changed? If they are the same racial patterns, how do you feel about that? If they are different racial patterns, what changed in how you developed friendships?

Friendships are as essential to our lives as our romantic relationships and fulfill a vital human need for connection. How we learn to grow and thrive in life is often shaped as much by our friendships as by our families. Our friends are with us through life's ups and downs. So when we seek to develop friendships with many different groups outside of our own race, we have the opportunity to deepen our understandings of how various racial groups experience life—often very differently from us.

RACE AND INTIMATE RELATIONSHIPS

Just as race and racism can influence how you develop friendships in different ways, the same goes for how it impacts your intimate relationships, from dating to long-term relationships. You likely learned implicit and explicit messages growing up, like whom you were supposed to date and whom you weren't. When my mom married my dad, her White family told her she "was on her own now" and looked down upon her partnership with a person of color. In addition to these messages, you know from the previous section that our neighborhoods, communities, and schools have long racial segregation histories. So even if you didn't get explicit messages like "Don't date outside of your race" or "You can date *this* race, but not *that* race," you might have gone to schools that weren't diverse, where there weren't many different racial groups. If so, you were likely still picking up those more subtle messages about whom you could develop intimate relationships with and whom you couldn't or should steer away from. We are also influenced by media messages that portray racially stereotyped messages about intimate relationships, such as consistent images of people dating only within their race (e.g., billboards, online dating sites).

In addition to the messages we receive about race and intimate relationships, when we are developing these relationships, we have our own internalized ideas of what we should or shouldn't do, whom we should or shouldn't be attracted to, and more. For instance, research has shown that people of color experience racism on online dating platforms. People may assume Latinx women are "curvy" based on stereotypes of what Latinx women look like, whereas Asian American women may be told they are "exotic," implying their perpetual foreign-ness. Some of the racial stereotypes people of color experience in developing relationships are even more egregious, such as being called a racial epithet or being told they are not attractive based on some White and Western conception of appearance and how bodies should be. On the other hand, White people may pursue partnerships with people of color because of their perceived "exoticness" or the features of their race that are "different," treating their partners in a fetishizing and objectifying manner.

If you are a person of color, you may have even more racial stereotypes to navigate through, depending on your sexual orientation (e.g., queer, questioning, lesbian, bisexual, aromantic, asexual, and more) and relational orientation (e.g., monogamous, polyamorous). If you are White, you may enter an online platform and never think twice about whether you will be stereotyped based on your race. One of my friends—let's call her Michiko—experienced this recently on an online dating site. Michiko is Asian American, and 80 percent of the messages she received included comments on her "exotic" features and assumptions about her sexual orientation (they assumed she was straight—she identifies as bisexual) and her relational orientation (they assumed she was monogamous—she's actually polyamorous).

If pursuing romantic relationships is important to you, encountering such stereotypes has an impact. Of course, my friend knew from previous experiences of more general racism that she might have racist experiences as she was dating online. And Michiko filtered out racialized comments about her racial identity when she received them. But even as Michiko was filtering those messages, she felt the burden those messages placed on her. Michiko ranged from feeling annoyed to angry to having old negative feelings come up about her racial features. A lot of times, Michiko feels safer dating within her race because she doesn't have to deal with all the stereotypes. She acknowledges this may be safer for her, but there is a cost as well. She would like to feel more freedom to date anyone she wishes to—that is, based on human connection and not just race.

If you are White, you might not think very much about how your race will influence your experiences dating and with romantic relationships, because you don't have these everyday instances of racism. Remember, that is the way that White privilege works—you can be oblivious to these racialized contexts. And if racism influences even the way we date and partner, it ultimately leads to how we develop our own families. It's so important to explore this, as you'll do in the next Racial Healing Practice, and challenge yourself to move beyond these stereotypes and restrictions.

RACIAL HEALING PRACTICE
Race, Dating, and Intimate Relationships

Take a moment to consider your history with attraction, dating, and intimate relationships and answer the questions below.

Growing up, what messages or stereotypes did you learn (from family, friends, schools, media) about dating and intimate relationships when it came to your race and the race of others?

_____

_____

_____

_____

_____

_____

Who was the first person to whom you remember being attracted? Was their race different from or similar to yours?

_____

_____

_____

_____

_____

_____

Over the course of your dating and intimate relationships, have you tended to date within your own race or outside of your race? Why do you think that is?

_____

_____

_____

_____

_____

_____

If you are White, how has your racial privilege shown up in your dating and intimate relationships (e.g., were you aware of or oblivious to your race and others)? If you are a person of color, what types of messages have you internalized about who you can and can't date or be in relationships with?

_____

_____

_____

_____

_____

_____

When you think of the racial patterns you have had in dating and intimate relationships, what are the top three patterns you would like to shift?

1. _____

2. _____

3. _____

What were the racial patterns you noticed in your dating and intimate relationships over your life thus far? Were the patterns different early on in your life compared to now? What type of emotions came up as you were writing about your experiences of race, dating, and intimate relationships? Were you surprised by any of the societal messages your received about who you could and should date in terms of race? Last question for now: as you answered these questions about dating and intimate relationships, did you find that your racial patterns were similar to those of your friendships you explored in the previous section, or different?

RACE AND SCHOOL AND PROFESSIONAL RELATIONSHIPS

There is a good deal of research that identifies how racism restricts employment opportunities, health, and housing for people of color (Stanford Center on Poverty and Inequality 2018). Due to racial segregation in neighborhoods, you may have attended schools with people who are racially similar to you. But even if you attended racially diverse schools where educators and school counselors prepared you for a racially diverse world, maybe you still hung out with people who shared your racial group and didn't interact much with others outside of your race. If you are White, maybe you tended to hang out with other White students. Or, as a person of color, maybe you needed to be able to connect with other students in your racial group to feel a sense of belonging, and you weren't able to do so—especially if you were attending a predominantly White school.

If this was true for you, you might have been in shock, whether you are White or a person of color, once you got to college or an employment setting where you were surrounded by people from many different racial groups. If so, you had to quickly learn how to interact with racial groups pretty different from you, and you likely had to confront some stereotypes you had of some racial groups for the first time ever—all while you were in a professional environment.

The tricky thing about school and work settings is that you have people who have learned stereotypes about their own racial groups and others, just like you have. Your academic or professional peers (and you) may be in a wide variety of racial identity development stages that you learned in chapter 3. So they may or may not be aware of their race, racial attitudes, biases, and so on. The extra tricky thing is that when you are the target of racism as a person of color in the workplace, it hurts, just as it does in friendships, dating, and intimate relationships. And, if you are White and not aware of how people of color are stereotyped in academic and work settings, you can intentionally or unintentionally hurt others with internalized, racist ideas of what it means to "act professional" in these settings.

Getting clear on what your racial patterns were like in schools and professional settings is an important strategy in healing from racism, since those patterns can drive racial stereotypes and attitudes you bring into the workplace. Engage in the next Racial Healing Practice to reflect on what you experienced growing up in school settings and how those experiences influence your decisions now about developing relationships at work.

RACIAL HEALING PRACTICE
Exploring How I Think about Race in Schools and Work

Dive in to the prompts below to identify how race has influenced your professional relationships at school and work.

Looking back at the schools you attended, what were the main messages you learned about your own race and the race of others?

_____

_____

_____

_____

_____

_____

In the schools you attended, did you hang out with folks within your own racial group, or did you interact with a diverse racial group?

_____

_____

_____

_____

_____

_____

Reflecting on your early work experiences, what were the racial groups you worked with the most? What was that like for you?

_____

_____

_____

_____

_____

_____

Across your work history, which racial groups have you never worked with, or only rarely worked with?

_____

_____

_____

_____

_____

_____

What racial stereotypes do you see at work? How do you respond (or not respond) to these racial stereotypes?

_____

_____

_____

_____

_____

_____

What racial conflicts have you seen or experienced at work? How do you respond (or not respond) to these racial conflicts?

_____

_____

_____

_____

_____

_____

When you think of the racial patterns you experienced at school and work, what are the top three patterns you would like to shift?

1. _____

2. _____

3. _____

What were the racial patterns you noticed in your school relationships over your life thus far? Were there any changes in these racial patterns from your first job to subsequent jobs? Next up, you will explore the impact of race in your relationships now.

TALKING ABOUT RACE IN YOUR CURRENT RELATIONSHIPS

As you start down the road of your racial healing journey and use all of the strategies in this workbook, you will begin to desire change in your current relationships with family and friends and at school or work. You are intentionally raising your race-consciousness, so you may attempt to raise their awareness as well. The results can range from awesome (e.g., good conversations, inspired to learn more) to not so awesome (e.g., mild difference in opinions to major disagreements leading to not speaking to one another). For example, I can challenge the internalized racism one of my uncles has, and still talk, joke, and laugh with him later whether we came to some agreement or not. It's really different with my other uncle. If we even get close to a topic of racism, it could result in a loud and unproductive screaming match. He's an important family member to me, so I decide to not broach these topics with him (although I do set clear boundaries about what he can say around me and not when it comes to race). On the other hand, I have an aunt who is just straight-up, unabashedly racist. I choose to *not* have a relationship with her, because I don't feel I can be in a relationship with her and also preserve my own integrity.

So, do you try to educate a friend, family member, or colleague when it looks like you might not agree on racial justice? It can be nerve-wracking to think about before it happens. You can also walk away from these conversations without speaking up and lose the opportunity to challenge racist ideas, which doesn't feel good either. I go back to these tips the Georgia Safe Schools Coalition (2009) used for educators talking about queer and trans students in anti-LGBTQ+ environments, and I apply these to a conversation about race:

- *Know your audience.* How you approach the conversation of race depends on the person you are talking to.

- *Be respectful.* Actively demonstrate respect, recognizing the person's thoughts and concerns.

- *Find common ground.* Even though you might disagree or are already in a disagreement, you probably have some shared ideas about race: (1) all people of color deserve to feel safe and supported in society, and (2) racism is a bad thing.

- *When applicable, share a personal experience.* From your work (re)educating yourself (chapter 3) and raising your race-consciousness (chapter 5), you've learned about history, data, and statistics of racism. Personal stories, though, can make this information more real, digestible, and heart-opening.

- *Be mindful of language.* Words are loaded with power, so breathe deeply, and be intentional about the words you use.

- *Develop a primary message and supporting messages.* This strategy will help you focus during the conversation. Your overall message should be clear, powerful, and effective, like "Racism affects everyone" or "Racist policies should be eliminated." Then, follow this primary message with supporting messages of data, personal stories, racial history, and so on.

- *Reframe the conversation.* When the person you are talking to goes on a tangent in the conversation, bring them back to your primary message.

- *Consider opposition framing.* Do your research and see what the "other side" believes. Design your primary and supporting messages accordingly.

- *Practice and prepare.* Practice with people you trust, like your friends, supportive family members, and your larger racial justice community (see chapter 10).

Do the next Racial Healing Practice to explore what this could "look like" with a person right now in your life. Once you've completed the activity, consider: How did it feel to practice effective messaging with your particular example of a conversation about race that went sideways? Was it pretty easy or tough to develop primary and supporting messages? Were there steps that you would like to practice more with this or other scenarios? Remember the story about my aunt; sometimes the conversations go badly, and it is okay to set a boundary and then get support for the resulting fallout that may occur. But also consider taking the risk to have the conversations about race—because only then can we get to challenge racist ideas within our own sphere of influence. And that influence adds up over time.

How did it feel to practice effective messaging with your particular example of a conversation about race that went sideways? Was it pretty easy or tough to develop primary and supporting messages? Were there steps that you would like to practice more with this or other scenarios? Remember the story about my aunt; sometimes the conversations go badly, and it is okay to set a boundary and then get support for the resulting fallout that may occur. But also consider taking the risk to have the conversations about race—because only then can we get to challenge racist ideas within our own sphere of influence. And that influence adds up over time.

RACIAL HEALING PRACTICE
Effective Messaging Strategies for
Conversations About Race

Think about the last conversation you had about race that didn't go so well. Write about that conversation a little here (e.g., topic, person, strategies you used, how you felt):

_____

_____

_____

_____

Now, you have a chance for a "do-over"! How could you use effective messaging techniques with this situation to keep you more focused and grounded?

Know your audience—What kind of approach was needed with this particular person(s)?

_____

_____

_____

Be respectful—How might you have demonstrated more respect?

_____

_____

_____

Find common ground—Was there an area of actual or potential agreement?

_____

_____

_____

When applicable, share a personal experience—What might you have shared?

_____

_____

_____

Be mindful of language—Was there language you could have used differently?

_____

_____

_____

Develop a primary message and supporting messages—Write these below.

1. _____

2. _____

Reframe the conversation—Did the person you spoke to take the conversation in a different direction? How could you have come back to your primary message?

_____

_____

_____

Consider opposition framing—What research could you have done to anticipate the other side?

_____

_____

_____

Practice and prepare—Who are your trusted folks and communities you could have practiced with?

_____

_____

_____

MAKING DECISIONS DIFFERENTLY IN DEVELOPING RELATIONSHIPS

So far, you have looked at the role race might have played as you developed personal and professional relationships in the past, and still may play as you build current and future relationships. You can interrupt these racial patterns and begin to develop relationships in a different way with this knowledge, because once you are aware of these you can make different decisions going forward.

For instance, for the majority of my life as a person of color, I was raised in predominantly White schools and neighborhoods. So you can guess that my friendship and dating patterns generally followed along the same racial lines, and you would be correct. However, my dad worked at a historically Black college and university (HBCU), and both my parents had deep friendships with Jewish folks. So despite the White neighborhoods and schools, my parent's social groups were both Black and White. There were very few Indian folks in their lives, as there were very few South Asians in New Orleans when I was growing up (and of course, we knew them all!)—so our Indian community was pretty tiny, as was my Indian friend group. As I have reflected on and increased my awareness of these racial patterns in my life, I have been able to make different decisions about how I develop relationships. For example, I wanted to break out of the limitations of these racialized patterns.

Now, I seek out Indian and South Asian friends. I also know I need good connections with mixed-race folks as friends and at work. This is important because I realized as a mixed-race person it wasn't okay that I wasn't accepted fully in both White and South Asian communities and experienced so much isolation. As I have developed more mixed-race relationships, I am actively building that racial home for myself with folks who get it. And I also have made it a goal to develop relationships in my personal and professional life with people who I rarely got to know growing up—like Latinx and indigenous people. And even though it's a given that I find familiarity and some comfort in my relationships with Black and Jewish Americans, I have also learned to look more deeply at the racialized assumptions I have internalized about these groups.

You learned about how to catch yourself in the flow of racism in relationships (chapter 6), and you will have the opportunity to explore how to interrupt patterns of racism from the position of being a racial ally and antiracist (chapter 9). For now, do the next Racial Healing Practice to explore how you can shift some of your racial patterns based on your new awareness and grow a more diverse relational group.

RACIAL HEALING PRACTICE
Making Decisions About Race Differently

In the previous Racial Healing Practices in this chapter, you ended each one identifying three patterns you wanted to shift. Take a look back over your answers and then complete the following:

What are the common racial patterns you noticed across your responses in this chapter? In other words, what are your racial comfort zones?

_____

_____

_____

_____

_____

_____

_____

_____

_____

_____

What are three next steps you could take right away to begin expanding the racial diversity of your personal and professional networks? (If you live or work in a racially homogenous place, think about how you can move beyond these homogenous communities or find diverse communities online.)

1. _____

2. _____

3. _____

What did you notice about your racial patterns overall in your personal and professional relationships? Was it challenging, easy, or somewhere in between to identify next steps for diversifying your personal and professional networks? Remember, it's okay to hang with and feel comfort with your own racial group. However, when you are developing skills to heal from racism, being around a diverse racial group of people in your personal and professional life is pretty important. It's the only way you actually learn close up about the various cultures and variations that exist within racial groups that might otherwise seem monolithic. That close-up learning is what also dispels unhelpful stereotypes that still bounce around in our minds in an unconscious way, unless we specifically challenge them. In addition, greater, more respectful contact between diverse groups of people is also what might help drive larger, systemic change down the line. And that is why knowing more about how race plays out in all of your relationships helps you do some healing.

RACIAL HEALING WRAP-UP

In this chapter you practiced the racial healing strategy of taking a deeper look at how racism influenced your personal and professional relationships. When you look at how you formed friendships and approached dating, intimate relationships, and relationships in school and at work, you discover ways that you can change those relationships to make them more diverse and more respectful. You will build on this work in the next chapter, developing skills in reclaiming your whole racial self through looking at other important identities (e.g., sexual orientation, class, gender identity) that intersect with your racial identity and influence how you navigate and challenge the system of racism.

CHAPTER 8

Reclaim Your Whole Racial Self

One of the major impacts of racism is that as a person of color or White person, you don't always get to explore other identities (e.g., sexual orientation, gender, class, disability, religion, age), some of which can intersect with your racial identity and mediate your racial privilege. *Intersectionality* is a theory developed by Black feminist scholars to get us thinking about the ways that multiple oppressions and privileges can overlap and have very real implications for how we experience racial oppressions and privileges (Bowleg 2008; Crenshaw 1989; Hill-Collins 1990; hooks 1989). For instance, White women have less power than White men. Having a higher social class can sometimes buffer the impact of racism for people of color. Experiencing deep poverty can blunt some aspects of White privilege. In this chapter, you will learn how healing from racism can be bolstered by exploring other identities that are important sources of transformation and liberation with your own particular intersections of privilege and oppression experiences.

WHO ARE YOU? NO, REALLY, WHO ARE YOU?

Moving through this workbook, you've thought a lot about your race as a person of color or as a White person. You've noticed that a deep exploration of your race helps you understand yourself more in everyday situations related to race. You've thought about who you thought you were in terms of your race, and you've uncovered racialized stereotypes and attitudes you may have internalized. As you have done this, you've had to consider who you *really* are and want to be in terms of your racial identity.

Similarly, your identities other than your race can influence you in a myriad of ways and deserve your attention and reflection. Just as your race affords you privilege or oppression within the system of racism, your other identities may also afford you privilege or oppression within an unjust system. For example:

- Your gender identity or sexual orientation may afford you privilege or oppression under the system of patriarchy (e.g., a Black, straight man can be heard differently in a business meeting than a Latina lesbian woman).

- Your class may afford you privilege or oppression under the system of capitalism. People of color who have class privilege can often buffer some of the effects of racism (e.g., having access to wealthier neighborhoods and more resourced schools), and White people who have a working class background or who grew up in deep poverty may question their ability to really "change" things when it comes to racism.

- Your age or ability may afford you privilege or oppression in a system that values and idealizes young and able bodies. White, young, able-bodied people can have lots of access to resources because of their multiple privileges, while Native American elders experience multiple oppressions of racism and ageism, in addition to ableism as their physical capabilities decline later in life.

Where do you fall with your multiple identities? Do the following Racial Healing Practice to find out. If you live outside of the US, you may need to adapt the exercise somewhat.

RACIAL HEALING PRACTICE
Taking a Pulse of My Multiple Identities

Have two different color pens, markers, or highlighters available. Below you'll find a table of social identities, systems of oppression, and related privilege and oppression identities that could intersect with your race, either in an additive fashion (contributing to the privilege your racial identity affords you or to the oppression that people with your racial identity encounter) or by serving as a buffer for a racial identity you might otherwise face more oppression for. For each row in the table, do the following:

- Use one color to circle the privilege status that applies to you.

- Use a different color to circle the oppression status that applies to you.

Social Identities, Privilege, and Oppression Outside of Race

Social Identity/System of Oppression	Privilege Status	Oppression Status
Race	White	Person of Color
Disability/Ableism	Able-bodied	Physical Disability, Cognitive Disability, Mental Health Disability
Gender/Sexism	Men, Cisgender	Women, Trans, Nonbinary, Genderqueer
Sexual Orientation	Heterosexual	LGBQ+, Polyamorous, Asexual, Aromantic
Religion	Christian	Muslim, Eastern, Pagan, Jewish, Hindu, Sikh, Buddhist, etc.
Social Class	Middle Class, Upper Class	Working Class, Poor
Age	Young Adults, Middle-Aged Adults	Children, Adolescents, Older Adults

As you went through the table and circled your identities, did you have more identities related to privilege or oppression, or an even mix of both? How did it feel to circle privilege identities? Did it feel different to circle oppression ones? Were there any identities you were unsure of or want to learn more about? Did you begin to think about how these multiple identities you have intersect with your race?

EXPLORING YOUR IDENTITIES

In this section, you will read about different realms of identity. Keep in mind that there are way more possible identities than those I will cover below. If reading about some of these identities feels like a "review" for you because of your previous knowledge and learning, I still encourage you to explore each one. Just as you have learned about your race, you can learn many, many more things about how to externalize internalized oppression or use privileges you have when you take the opportunity to slow down and reflect on their impacts on your life. On the other hand, if some of these identities are new to you, this overview can be a jumping-off point for you to further your learning (I provide resources for this at the end of the chapter). Regardless, know that the exploration of your identities below is *in relation to your racial identity*.

After the description of each identity and related privilege and oppression experiences, you'll do a Racial Healing Practice to explore how that realm of identity intersects with your racial identity, and whether it adds to your privilege, buffers your privilege, or adds to your oppression. You'll also get a chance to reflect on how you see that particular identity intersecting with race for others.

(Dis)ability and Ableism

Your *(dis)ability status* (or *(dis)ability identity*) refers to the extent to which you live with physical, mental, and cognitive disabilities. *Ableism* is the system that privileges people who are able-bodied and disadvantages people living with these disabilities. Some disabilities are present from birth (e.g., autism, cerebral palsy, dyslexia, learning disabilities), but others can evolve over time and can range in length, progression, and severity (e.g., wearing glasses, movement challenges, short-term wheelchair use). Just like all social identities, when race intersects with ability, racial privilege can be additive to another privilege (as when one is White *and* able-bodied); or it can buffer an oppression identity (as when one is White and has a disability); or it might be additive to an oppression identity (as when a person of color also has a disability identity). Below are examples of how ableism and racism can intersect:

- An Asian American child living with autism is ostracized at school for both racial and disability reasons.

- A Black adolescent boy living with depression is not referred to the school counselor by his majority White teachers because they assume he is "lazy" and "doesn't want to engage in learning."

- A White child living with a learning disability benefits from her White parents' advocacy for her to receive needed school resources to support her learning.

- A Latinx college student living with cerebral palsy experiences rejection due to racial and disability reasons.

- A Native American woman was recently diagnosed with a brain tumor and spends her life savings on urgent and necessary medical care. In the hospital, she hears her nurse make a racist comment about her tribe, and there is not another hospital facility near her that she can access.

RACIAL HEALING PRACTICE
(Dis)ability + Race = My Intersecting
Identities of Privilege and Oppression

Write a little about how you think your (dis)ability intersects with your race.

_____

_____

_____

_____

How do you think others perceive your (dis)ability intersecting with your race?

_____

_____

_____

How do you think you perceive the (dis)ability of *others* intersecting with their race?

_____

_____

_____

As you work to reduce ableism—either as a White person by using your racial privilege or as a person of color by using your own and others' experiences of racism—what experiences, knowledge, or understandings do you need to keep in mind in terms of your (dis)ability intersecting with your race?

_____

_____

_____

Gender and Sexism

There's a lot to say about gender. But in this section, we'll keep it somewhat simple: You have a sex you were assigned at birth (typically female or male; there is also an intersex identity, which is a combination of multiple anatomical structures, not just those assigned to females and males). You also have a gender, that internal sense of who you are (e.g., man, woman, another gender, no gender). Your gender may be in alignment with your sex assigned at birth, and the term used for this identity is *cisgender*. If the sex you were assigned at birth does not align with your gender identity, you may identify as trans, gender nonconforming, nonbinary, genderqueer, some other gender, or no gender at all. You also have an expression of your gender, which might include your clothing, hairstyle, and other ways of expressing yourself in the world; labels for gender expression include feminine, masculine, androgynous, none of these, or all of these.

Gender intersects with race in many different ways related to privilege and oppression. Racism can moderate some aspects of gender privilege—for example, cisgender male privilege can be reduced by the racial identity of a person of color (Latinx cisgender man) or enhanced by an additive privilege (White cisgender man). Here are a few examples of how sexism and racism can intersect:

- A Native American cisgender woman is asked if she lives on a reservation.

- A Black trans man is seen as a "threat" and is assumed to be a criminal by the police.

- A Latinx cisgender woman is asked if she can dance the salsa.

- An Asian American trans woman is told she is "exotic looking."

- A White cisgender man has increased access to resources, like higher pay at work.

RACIAL HEALING PRACTICE
Gender + Race = My Intersecting
Identities of Privilege and Oppression

Write a little about how you think your gender intersects with your race.

_____

_____

_____

_____

How do you think others perceive your gender intersecting with your race?

_____

_____

_____

How do you think you perceive the gender of *others* intersecting with their race?

_____

_____

_____

As you work to use your racial privilege as a White person to reduce racism or as you work as a person of color to reduce racism you experience in the world around you, what experiences, knowledge, or understandings do you need to keep in mind in terms of your gender intersecting with your race?

_____

_____

_____

_____

Sexual Orientation and Heterosexism

Your *sexual orientation* (sometimes called your *affectional orientation*) refers to your sexuality (e.g., straight, queer, questioning, lesbian, bisexual, gay, pansexual, polysexual, asexual), and can include your patterns of partnership or relational orientation (e.g., monogamous, polyamorous). *Straight* tends to refer to your attractions to people who don't share your gender identity, while other words refer to attractions including to those who share your gender identity. For example, men can be attracted to men (gay), women can be attracted to women (lesbian), and people can have attractions to multiple genders (lesbian, pansexual, polysexual, queer). People can also be exploring their attractions to genders (questioning), or they may not experience sexual attraction (asexual).

Heterosexism is the system where those who identify as straight and monogamous have privilege. For instance, straight and monogamous people are less frequently judged, pathologized, and exoticized. Their relationships are more recognized as valuable to the state, and therefore they receive the informal benefits tied to marriage and monogamous relationships more easily than those who are not straight and monogamous. (Even though queer people have legal rights now, they may still miss out on the wedding shower being thrown by work colleagues and they may feel it's unsafe to share about their marriage to family members.)

Like other identities, your racial privilege or oppression can be buffered or multiplied by your sexual orientation privilege or oppression. Here are a few examples:

- An Asian American cisgender polyamorous person experiences both racism and prejudice related to her relational orientation.

- A White trans gay man who is monogamous has multiple privileges of being White, male, and monogamous.

- A Black cisgender lesbian who is monogamous experiences multiple oppressions of racism, heterosexism, and sexism, but has privilege afforded to monogamy.

- A Latinx cisgender queer person who is polyamorous experiences multiple oppressions of racism, heterosexism, and anti-polyamory prejudice.

- A Native American trans person who is asexual experiences racism as well as bias within and outside of their family because they are asexual.

RACIAL HEALING PRACTICE
Sexual Orientation + Race = My Intersecting Identities of Privilege and Oppression

Write a little about how you think your sexual orientation intersects with your race.

_____
_____
_____
_____

How do you think others perceive your sexual orientation intersecting with your race?

_____
_____
_____

How do you think you perceive the sexual orientation of *others* intersecting with their race?

_____
_____
_____

As you work to reduce heterosexism—either as a White person by using your racial privilege or as a person of color by using your own and others' experiences of racism—what experiences, knowledge, or understandings do you need to keep in mind in terms of your sexual orientation intersecting with your race?

_____
_____
_____
_____

Religion and Religious Privilege

Religious identity (sometimes called *spiritual identity*) refers to the extent to which you identify or don't identify with religion or spirituality—in essence your belief in whether God or some other higher power exists. Christian privilege is a hallmark of religious/spiritual privilege, and is present in many countries in the West (e.g., US, Europe, Latin America). However, religious privilege can look very different depending on the area of the world you are in (e.g., in India, a predominantly Hindu country, Christians, Muslims, and Sikhs lack religious privilege). In addition, people can enact religious privilege when they assume those under the atheist umbrella (e.g., agnostic, nonbeliever) are "wrong" or "misguided." Let's look at how this can play out:

- A Native American person who identifies as atheist is discriminated against for her racial and nonreligious identities.

- A Black person who identifies as Muslim faces oppression for both her racial identity and her religious identity at the same time.

- A Latinx person who identifies as Buddhist experiences racism in society and also religious bias within his own community because of her religious identity.

- An Asian American who identifies as Christian is exoticized by White people for her culture and experiences microinsults when she discloses she doesn't practice an Eastern-based religion.

- A White person who identifies as Jewish has White privilege and also experiences anti-Semitism.

RACIAL HEALING PRACTICE
Religious Identity + Race = My Intersecting Identities of Privilege and Oppression

Write a little about how you think your religious identity intersects with your race.

_____

_____

_____

_____

How do you think others perceive your religious identity intersecting with your race?

_____

_____

_____

How do you think you perceive the religious identity of *others* intersecting with their race?

_____

_____

_____

As you work to reduce religious privilege—either as a White person by using your racial privilege or as a person of color by using your own and others' experiences of racism—what experiences, knowledge, or understandings do you need to keep in mind in terms of your religious identity intersecting with your race?

_____

_____

_____

_____

Social Class and Classism

Social class is an identity that refers to the amount of financial resources you have and the environments and social circles you travel in as a result. This identity may seem pretty straightforward—you either have more than enough resources (wealthy, upper class, owning class), enough resources (middle class), or not enough resources (deep poverty, working class) when it comes to money. However, your class can change throughout your life. For example, your family might have been upper class when you were growing up, but then transitioned to lower class or poverty due to unexpected medical bills and expenses or lack of access to strong educational systems.

Your education level can also be a part of your social class. Your social class can dictate the level of conventional education you do or do not receive, for instance having little education or obtaining a GED, high school diploma, or vocational certificate. You may have more class privilege if you have an associate's degree, bachelor's degree, or graduate degree because your education may afford you greater access to financial resources. On the other hand, you may go into debt as you access higher levels of education, which can reduce your education and class privilege in terms of your finances. However, even in these circumstances, your education level may provide you with resources and information to address challenges, like debt, that someone without that education does not have. Class privilege also manifests beyond the social class you were in growing up. Employment (e.g., promotions, career ladder) and geographic location (e.g., moving from a rural area with few employment resources to an urban or suburban area with lots of employment opportunities) can also influence your class identity. Social class and education privilege can get super-complicated! Look at the identity intersections below of classism and racism to see the complexity of these multiple identities:

- A Black person who was raised in poverty but receives a scholarship to a top university now has access to financial and social class resources. People assume she is wealthy because of the university she attends, but her scholarship pays for tuition and boarding only and she struggles to pay her phone bill.

- A White person who recently came to the US as a refugee is working class. He benefits from White privilege (people assume he has been in the US for multiple generations), but he is finding it difficult to find employment.

- A Native American person is from an upper class family but did not graduate from high school. She has access to wealth, but she is scared to apply to college because she thinks she isn't smart enough to go.

- An Asian American person from a middle class family has high amounts of university loans. As he seeks employment, he experiences racial discrimination and his family cannot assist because they are living paycheck to paycheck.

- A Latinx person from a wealthy class pursues her PhD. She experiences racial microaggressions, but she is able to be a full-time doctoral student taking on no student loans.

RACIAL HEALING PRACTICE
Social Class + Race = My Intersecting
Identities of Privilege and Oppression

Write a little about how you think your social class intersects with your race.

_____

_____

_____

_____

How do you think others perceive your social class intersecting with your race?

_____

_____

_____

How do you think you perceive the social class of *others* intersecting with their race?

_____

_____

_____

As you work to reduce classism—either as a White person by using your racial privilege or as a person of color by using your own and others' experiences of racism—what experiences, knowledge, or understandings do you need to keep in mind in terms of your social class intersecting with your race?

_____

_____

_____

Age, Adultism, and Ageism

Age identity refers to your chronological age or the age you are perceived as in society. When it comes to age identity, there are a couple of systems of oppression operating. *Adultism* is the oppression of children, adolescents, and those who are perceived as young in society. Adultism manifests in the idea that children and adolescents must be controlled and don't have agency over their own bodies and decisions. *Ageism* is the oppression of older people by young adults and middle-aged adults. Within ageism, older adults can be treated as having declining value, and their contributions to society can be overlooked. Let's look at some examples of the intersection of age and race with regard to privilege and oppression:

- A Native American older person is fired for "moving too slow."

- A Latinx older adult has not received a raise in multiple years despite excellent performance reviews.

- An Asian American older faculty member at a retiree party is assumed to be one of the waitstaff.

- A Black adolescent in a predominantly White school leads a Black Lives Matter protest and is labeled a "troublemaker."

- A White trans child's gender pronouns are not used or respected by educators in their school.

RACIAL HEALING PRACTICE
Age + Race = My Intersecting Identities of Privilege and Oppression

Write a little about how you think your age identity intersects with your race. Note your privilege and oppression identities related to adultism and ageism.

_____

_____

_____

_____

How do you think others perceive your age intersecting with your race?

_____

_____

_____

How do you think you perceive the age of _others_ intersecting with their race?

_____

_____

_____

As you work to reduce adultism and ageism—either as a White person by using your racial privilege or as a person of color by using your own and others' experiences of racism—what experiences, knowledge, or understandings do you need to keep in mind in terms of your age intersecting with your race?

_____

_____

_____

_____

There are way more social identities than we had space for you to explore in this chapter, but we did cover some of the major ones. In your exploration of some of your multiple social identities other than race, did you identify intersections to learn more about or to value more? Every time I dive into reflection on my multiple identities, I find new ways I want to be and grow. As a person of color who identifies religiously as a Sikh, I think about how significant this intersection is for me. Everything I learned about social justice growing up came from my mom and dad's messages in raising me in this religion. The central tenets of Sikhism include doing community service (*seva*), seeking justice for all (the founder, Guru Nanak, fought against India's caste system), and uplifting women's status in society as important and valuable. My dad and mom drilled these religious ideas into my head from early on in my life. I probably wouldn't be writing this workbook without the strength of this intersection. So my experiences of race were truly buffered by my religious upbringing in many ways. Standing up for others and myself is strongly linked to my religious identity. I endeavor to find ways to use my religious privilege to make spaces more affirming of atheist folks (like not assuming everyone wants to pray or identifies with a religion). On the other hand, although my religious identity may have privilege in relation to atheists, it definitely doesn't in the US, where Christian privilege is predominant. I still have a lot of healing to do in relation to negative messages and questions I received growing up about being Sikh and about my dad wearing a turban, which multiplied many of the negative messages I received about my race and skin color.

I also think of the intersection of my social class, which changed significantly over my life, with my race. We grew up without much money, but I had various scholarships to schools and universities that gave me tremendous educational privilege, which then allowed me to pursue graduate education and my doctorate. As a person of color, I definitely had negative experiences throughout my education. At the same time, my educational and growing class privilege provided buffering against that racism. I couldn't totally "opt out" of the racism of course, but I had options, thanks to my educational and class privilege. For instance, I had the freedom to choose places of employment and social environments in which I might experience less racism using my related class and educational privilege.

Do the last Racial Healing Practice in this chapter to explore how the most salient privilege and oppression identities in your life intersect with your race.

RACIAL HEALING PRACTICE
My Most Important Identity Intersections with My Race

What are the three most important identities to you other than your race? Write those here. Refer to the earlier table in this chapter if you need a quick refresher.

1. _____

2. _____

3. _____

How do these three identities influence how you feel about your race?

_____

_____

_____

_____

How do these three identities multiply your privilege or buffer your oppression?

_____

_____

_____

_____

How can you value these three identities further and be more aware and conscious about them on your healing from racism journey?

_____

_____

_____

_____

What was it like for you to explore the intersections between your racial identity and other social identities (ability, gender, sexual orientation, ability religion, social class, age)? Were some intersections easier or tougher to think about as you wrote about them? Can you begin to see an overall picture of how these social identities intersect all together with your race and related privilege and oppression experiences you have? I find that the more conscious I am of these intersections, the more I learn overall about myself as a racial being. For instance, I spent a lot of time early in my life thinking *only* about racism and heterosexism as a queer person of color experiencing these marginalizations. But I have a good deal of social class privilege—I am married, own a house, have a savings account, and have multiple advanced degrees. So, even though I am a queer person of color, I am buffered to some degree from racism and heterosexism by my class privilege alone. It doesn't mean I don't get hurt by these systems of oppression, but I can also use my social class privilege to be a stronger racial ally (next up in chapter 9) and make important social change for communities that don't have that same privilege (more on this in chapter 10).

RACIAL HEALING WRAP-UP

In this chapter, you explored your social identities and their intersections with your racial identity. You also learned about the system of injustice (e.g., sexism, classism, ableism) as well as who has privilege and who doesn't in this unjust system. I encourage you to keep learning more about how these multiple identities intersect because these junctions can change and be fluid. Knowing more about these intersections in your own life and others' also helps strengthen your advocacy on larger levels. As you reclaim your whole self—racial identity and all your identities—you have a powerful healing strategy to keep refining. You are also poised to better engage as a racial ally and antiracist, which is what the next chapter is all about.

CHAPTER 9

Be a Racial Ally

As you commit more and more to challenging the system of racism and its effects on others and yourself, you likely will run across the idea of being an ally. A racial *ally* is someone who actively supports others who are experiencing racial injustice, prejudice, and discrimination. If you have privilege of any kind—from being White, straight, cisgender, or able-bodied or having enough or more than enough financial resources, and more—the key idea within allyship is that you are using the privilege you have to refute oppression.

If you are White, being a racial ally means that you use your White privilege to challenge everyday racism. Being a White racial ally means you have worked hard to become more attuned to the ways that racism can show up, overtly or covertly, within yourself and within your relationships. You signal to White friends and colleagues that you will take action to speak out and act when it comes to racism, and you signal to people of color that you are an advocate.

If you are a person of color, you may not have racial privilege, but you do have the opportunity to be a racial ally to yourself and other people of color. For example, if in my work I become aware of a policy that contains covert racism that affects people of color, I speak up against it. My social class plays a big part in what I do as a person of color too. I use my social or professional position and the resources and respect afforded to me as a professor and administrator to do so. I am working as an ally for those who will be affected by the policy, in addition to acting on my own behalf. Whether I am successful or not in my advocacy, I signal to other people of color that I am attuned to the ways racism can present itself. I also signal to White folks that I am a racial ally to myself—I won't be silent when it comes to issues of race.

In this chapter, you will explore the idea of acting as an ally. You will even have the opportunity to critique the word a little bit; the concept of *allyship* is not without its problems, especially as some people with privilege practice it. Along the way you will be developing the racial healing strategy of taking action for yourself and others as a racial ally.

WHAT "ALLY" REALLY MEANS

Especially when you start getting engaged in larger movements working toward dismantling racism (see chapter 10), you may hear the word "ally" used pretty frequently as a noun and as a verb, as in the following definitions and examples:

Ally (noun): an individual who works as an advocate for people of color facing racism

- "I'm working on being a White ally."

- "I believe this is work White allies need to take on, not people of color."

- "I need support from White allies." (spoken by a person of color to a White person)

- "I want to be an ally to myself as a Latinx person and speak up on this racial issue."

Ally (verb): the act of speaking up for oneself or others when facing individual or structural racism

- "I want to ally with you on this racial issue." (spoken by a White person to a person of color)

- "As a Black person, I am allying with myself and my community when I challenge this anti-Black policy."

- "The school administration needs to ally with faculty of color so important issues of racism are addressed."

You get the idea. Although even the Urban Dictionary hasn't caught up with this specific use of the word "ally" in a racialized context, it's a very real issue you want to explore as a healing from racism strategy. This is primarily because being a strong racial ally means you are moving beyond awareness that racism is real and is displayed all the time to actions that stop racism in its tracks—not just for yourself, but for those around you. Do the next Racial Healing Practice to explore the actions of being a racial ally.

RACIAL HEALING PRACTICE
Becoming a Racial Ally

Whether being a racial ally is a new idea to you or whether it's something you have been doing for a while, it's helpful to reflect on what it means to you personally to be a racial ally. Remember that whether you are White or a person of color, you can be a racial ally to your own race and to others outside of your race.

Write about three times you have been a racial ally in the past.

1. _____

_____

_____

2. _____

_____

_____

3. _____

_____

_____

Write about three opportunities you have right now to be a racial ally (e.g., at work or school, with your family or friends, in your community).

1. _____

_____

_____

2. _____

_____

_____

3. _____

_____

_____

Write about three times it has been tough to be a racial ally. If you can't think of three times you've practiced allyship, think about three reasons you might be apprehensive about being a racial ally in the future.

1. _____

_____

_____

2. _____

_____

_____

3. _____

_____

_____

Did you notice any common challenges you have faced as a racial ally? What might be some next steps you can make to take advantage of the opportunities to be a racial ally? Hold on to these thoughts, because next you'll look even closer at some of the tricky aspects of being a racial ally.

THE DOS AND DON'TS OF RACIAL ALLYSHIP

One of the tricky things about being a racial ally is the question of whether you can really appoint yourself as a racial ally, because allyship inherently involves being in a position of privilege. It involves demonstrating your privilege on another's behalf—an exercise of power that the other person may consider condescending to or diminishing of them. Especially if you are White, this is an interesting and important question to unpack. Even if you are a person of color and allying with your own community of color, there are so many differences among individuals within communities of color (e.g., gender identity, sexual orientation, social class, and disability, among others, as you explored in chapter 8) that it is still important to ask yourself about the utility of appointing yourself as an ally.

Self-appointment of allyship can mean we are off the mark of being a good racial ally. Rather, when you are doing the ongoing, everyday work of unlearning racism in your own life, supporting others when there is racial injustice, and seeking to learn about and grow in your efforts toward reducing the impact of racism in the world, then you are more grounded in the actual intention of being a true racial ally—a stance from which the most helpful actions of allyship could flow. Here are some guidelines for engaging in helpful and healthy allying in a community and confronting racial discrimination and oppression.

Being a racial ally *does* mean:

- *Staying humble.* Humility is the most important value to keep in mind when you are exercising the privilege, as allies often do, of acting on another's behalf. Cultivating humility as a racial ally means learning to look at the context of each situation in which you find yourself tempted to act to see what would be most helpful for the person you want to ally with or advocate for, so you can avoid putting that person at risk or painting yourself as a savior in a way the person would find disrespectful.

- *Apologizing when you get it "wrong"—and not overapologizing to the point that the person feels they need to take care of you!* Being a racial ally means you are going to make mistakes and stumble along the way. As people committed to working to end racism and foster healing from racism, we find this tough to think about because the issues related to racial injustice are so important and pressing. However, racial allies do and will get some things wrong. Rather than overapologizing or (worse) not apologizing at all or avoiding the mistake, racial allies learn to lean into the discomfort of making a mistake, make a simple apology, and recommit to their own further growth and learning about being a better racial ally.

- *Being a good listener.* Learning to listen well is one of the toughest things to do when it comes to racism. Many times it's more helpful to step back (especially if you are more of an extrovert or like to talk a lot) and listen to the needs of people of color about racial injustice or listen to understand the best ways to work with fellow White or people of color community members to foster more awareness and action on issues of racism.

- *Believing the experiences that people of color have.* For White folks, this may seem straightforward, but people of color often have their experiences minimized or denied when they share how racism shows up in their lives. For people of color, racial allyship means checking in to see where your internalized racism might be keeping you from fully supporting, hearing, and validating the stories of racism from fellow people of color.

- *Continuing to educate yourself about racism.* It's easy to think we have learned everything there is to know about racism. A healthy approach to racial allyship is to know that there is always more to learn. For White folks—this is particularly important—don't ask or expect folks of color to educate you on an issue. Ongoing learning can include attending workshops, trainings, and street protests, as well as visiting libraries and learning about racial issues online.

- *Connecting with other racial allies.* For White people, this might mean participating in or facilitating a group exploring White privilege and sustainable ways to take everyday action. For people of color, this might also mean connecting with other folks of color and learning about the divergent identities and perspectives that can exist within communities of color so that there is attention to being inclusive of people of color from all backgrounds.

Being a racial ally *does not* mean:

- *Appointing yourself as a racial ally.* Whatever you do, do not present yourself as the "all-knowing" White person or all-knowing person of color.

- *Pausing your racial allyship.* Healthy racial allies don't overcommit and overextend themselves past their boundaries, but they also don't stop or hesitate when it comes to challenging racial oppression.

- *Participating in "call-out" culture.* This refers to the act of shaming and blaming people who are unaware of their White supremacy. Now, this doesn't mean that racial allies ignore these situations—they just realize that the shame-and-blame game doesn't work that well. Racial allies focus their efforts on more sustainable challenges to racism and use their power to identify more helpful ways to challenge racism.

- *Talking about how you are a racial ally at every chance you get.* People will know you are a solid racial ally from your thoughts, feelings, and actions when it comes to challenging racism.

- *Thinking that you have all the answers to solving racism or that you are more enlightened than your fellow White people or people of color.* Arrogance is certainly not on the racial ally menu, but you will see this commonly. The reality is we are all doing our best to change a structural system of privilege and oppression that is much bigger than any of us. And the ways we might respond to that system may change from year to year or situation to situation. So, allyship requires humility, flexibility, and the willingness to keep learning and reevaluating what you think you know, especially when you encounter other allies or people of color who tell you the way you're practicing allyship may be backfiring.

- *Avoiding feelings of grief and loss.* Racial allyship is rewarding *and* tough work, and a range of emotions might come up. When it is rewarding, you may experience excitement, hope, fear, and anticipation, sometimes all at the same time, related to potential change and racial justice. When it is tough, it is helpful to know what stage of grief you are in (look back at chapter 4). For instance, you might be squarely in the anger stage when you are advocating for someone. Anger is an important emotion that can be overwhelming. Being in touch with your anger in a healthy way can help you use that anger to advocate and set boundaries as an ally. On the other hand, you might be in the depression stage, where feelings of sadness are very present. Knowing that and being able to express that sadness as an advocate with people you trust—and sometimes with the people you are advocating with as a racial ally— can help you be more effective.

There is a lot more to be said about what being a racial ally is and is not. To delve into this further, do the next Racial Healing Practice below.

RACIAL HEALING PRACTICE
Applying the Dos of Racial Allyship

Whether you are White and identifying ways to use your privilege more effectively to challenge injustice or whether you are a person of color looking to ally more with your fellow people of color and communities of color, being a racial ally requires ongoing awareness and practice. Respond to the following questions to identify how to grow your awareness of the practice of racial allyship.

What are three ways that you can educate yourself about racism in an ongoing manner?

1. _____

_____

_____

2. _____

_____

_____

3. _____

_____

_____

What are three ways you can become a good listener as a racial ally?

1. _____

_____

_____

2. _____

_____

_____

3. _____

_____

_____

What are three ways you can connect with other racial allies as a White person or person of color?

1. _____

_____

_____

2. _____

_____

_____

3. _____

_____

_____

What are three instances in the past when, as a racial ally, you could have apologized when you got it "wrong" (and not over-apologized to the point the person felt they needed to take care of you)?

1. _____

_____

_____

2. _____

_____

_____

3. _____
   _____
   _____

What are three ways you can endeavor to believe the experiences that people of color have?

1. _____
   _____
   _____

2. _____
   _____
   _____

3. _____
   _____
   _____

As you wrote about the "dos" of racial allyship, did you notice any ways the "don'ts" could show up in your responses? Were there some "dos" that felt easier than others? Not only is that okay, but it's also really important to notice your growing edges (i.e., how you are breaking through your fears). It's through working on our growing edges as White folks and folks of color that we can become stronger and stronger racial allies.

HOW DO I TAKE ACTION IN THE MOMENT AS A RACIAL ALLY?

As you have learned, so much of developing into a strong racial ally means practice, practice, and then even more practice. Sometimes you get being a racial ally right—and sometimes your best intentions can go sideways. For example, when you hear a racist joke, as a White person or person of color, what do you do? Often, these instances of racism—even if you know they exist—take you by surprise, making it hard to find your voice and identify your next steps. Maybe you are so shocked that you don't say anything, and then beat yourself up about it later. So planning for how you can intervene is critically important to head more in the direction of being an effective racial ally.

Having said this, not every racial ally will take the same exact actions in response to an incident or systemic aspect of racism. Much of what you do and don't do as a racial ally has to do with your personality, your past history, and your individual circumstances. When it comes to your personality, if you are more extroverted, you may find it easier to speak up in the moment when you see racist acts occurring. If you are more introverted, you may need to identify concrete strategies to support you in speaking out in a group or request a one-on-one conversation with a person who has perpetrated racism. The point is that no matter what your personality is, you don't let racism go unchecked, but you also know what is the best way for you as an individual to respond. When it comes to your past history, learning to be a racial ally is influenced by whether you've experienced certain racist or traumatic incidents in the past. Your circumstances, such as your particular level of access to privilege or safety to act in a given moment, will also influence how you respond as a racial ally.

Another way to become a more effective racial ally is by increasing your awareness about your boundaries and connecting your boundaries to what I call your comfort zone, your growth zone, and your danger zone:

Comfort zone. This is a place of action and inaction on racism. You are able to respond to some things but not other things when it comes to racial incidents and systems. You can be effective in your comfort zone. For instance, a person of color may be able to challenge racism by speaking with others and getting support in how to take the next steps of action as an ally. However, they may not be ready or able to speak out and confront the person enacting the racism. Your comfort zone is vitally important in taking action against racism. However, there are plenty of times when I am in my comfort zone that I let the opportunities to intervene when it comes to racism pass me by, so that's the danger of your comfort zone.

Growth zone. This is a zone where you are literally less comfortable than your comfort zone. You aren't past your boundaries in a danger zone, but you focus your actions as a racial ally from your growing edge. As a White racial ally, you remain open when it comes to learning more about your own internalized racism and the racism of others, but you also seek to identify new ways of acting in a variety of racialized situations and you take risks to stand up for others. Your growth zone is essentially an ongoing active space of learning and growth. You can't live here 100% of the time, but you aim to increase the time you are in the growth zone more and more to enhance the effectiveness of your racial allyship.

Danger zone. This is the scary zone past your boundaries. You aren't effective in this zone. When an incident of racism or a racist structure brings you to your danger zone, you may become defensive; you may minimize the existence of racism in a variety of racialized situations, because the risk of acknowledging it feels too great; and you may shut down when it comes to talking about race. In this zone, you lose the opportunity for growth or comfort. Typically, when we are in the danger zone, we are trying to head back as soon as we can for the comfort zone. If you are White, it could mean you aren't open to exploring your mistakes, misguided intentions, or opportunities for growth as a racial ally. As a person of color, being in your danger zone could mean you are exhausted from experiences of racism and need to move into your comfort zone and connect with people who can support you; it could also entail a great possibility of verbal, physical, or some other type of harm. I know I am making the danger zone sound terrible. It's not an ideal stage—and no growth takes place here—but it is a stage for which I have developed a great respect. Moving out of our comfort zone to our growth zones as racial allies requires risk. We are doing something different when it comes to racism. And as we take these risks, we might inadvertently dip our toes into the danger zone. I'm not saying we should hang out in the danger zone or ignore it. But I am saying we should be aware that as we learn to become an effective racial ally and take these risks, we may be dancing pretty closely to the danger zone. I see the danger zone as one to grow your awareness about: what does it feel like when you are in it, and what support do you need from yourself and others to move out of this zone?

Do the next Racial Healing Practice to dive into your comfort, growth, and danger zones so you can increase your awareness of what it looks and feels like for you to be in these zones.

RACIAL HEALING PRACTICE
Knowing My Comfort, Growth, and
Danger Zones as a Racial Ally

Now that you know a little bit about how being in different zones can shift the effectiveness of your racial allyship, take some time to reflect on how your comfort, growth, and danger zones show up in your own life.

Comfort Zone—Write about a time as a racial ally where you were somewhat effective in your efforts, but you could have been more effective.

_____

_____

_____

_____

_____

_____

Growth Zone—Use the example you just wrote about, and now write about how you might have moved more toward your growth zone in this situation. What are the actions you might have taken if you had a "re-do" of that same situation? How could you have made your racial allyship more effective?

_____

_____

_____

_____

_____

_____

_____

Danger Zone—Again, take the same instance you wrote about in your comfort zone above. What about that situation would push you into your danger zone? Think about the things that might make you shut down, numb out, get defensive, and so on, whether as a White or privileged person or as a disadvantaged person or person of color. What would you need in terms of support from yourself and others to move you out of that danger zone?

_____

_____

_____

_____

_____

_____

Hang on to what you learned about yourself and your comfort, growth, and danger zones, because being a racial ally will mean circling in and out of these zones. Knowing your typical responses and actions will help you be more aware of how to shift into your growth zone and take action against racism and minimize your times in the less helpful (but still very real) comfort and danger zones.

IS "ALLY" THE RIGHT WORD? WHAT ABOUT "ACCOMPLICE" OR "CO-CONSPIRATOR"?

Now that you have explored being a racial ally in some depth, it's time to ask yourself if "ally" is the right word for you. I'm not saying you should throw the word away, but as you grow within your racial allyship, you may decide that the word "ally" can keep you at a distance from racism. For instance, you may experience that your racial allyship is effective, but because you aren't experiencing that particular racial microaggression or macroaggression, you might be falling into a "savior" role as a racial ally. I see the savior role not as actual allyship, but more so as forgetting that we are *all* impacted by racism.

As a White racial ally, you may more deeply explore how to use your racial privilege to make change when it comes to racism. In this regard, a word like "accomplice" or "co-conspirator" may feel like a better fit for what you are actually doing as a racial ally. An example I heard recently helps put this in perspective. Let's say there is a movement to take down a Confederate flag, and people of color are leading the protest but also being targeted by police. As a White racial ally, you decide in collaboration with the leaders that you can use your White privilege to keep the people of color safer by using your body to literally "get in the way" of the oppressive acts of the police. In this regard, you are literally becoming a different kind of racial ally—one who can use your White privilege to make an immediate impact. In this way, a word like "accomplice" or "co-conspirator" reflects your commitment to this movement that is challenging the upholding of Confederate monuments. Well, Bree Newsome, Black woman activist, did exactly this. She took down the South Carolina Confederate flag while supported by White racial co-conspirator and accomplice Jimmy Tyson.

For people of color racial allies, it's the same idea, but there are obviously different risks involved because systems of racism are built to disadvantage people of color. Let's say you are a university administrator, and a racist speaker is slated to talk on campus. Students of color decide to protest this event. You know that students don't have as much power as you do as an administrator, so as an accomplice you decide to take part in their activism and show up as a witness. You attend their planning meetings and offer support, including insight into the current administration and considerations in dealing with campus police and potential violence from those supporting the speakers. The idea of being an accomplice and a co-conspirator as a person of color is that you are putting something on the line for racial justice—your own self. You are no longer safe in terms of distance, and there are potential consequences you are knowingly risking in doing so. You may decide that you want to use "allyship" when you are taking action to address racism within the structures of society in which racist acts occur—like interrupting racial microaggressions and racist speech. On the other hand, you might want to use "accomplice" or "co-conspirator" as the terms for the actions you take to combat racism through direct challenge to or subversion of racist structures and institutions, such as changing racist policies, working on systemic change, and supporting social protests and direct social change actions. When you use "accomplice" or "co-conspirator," you get closer to street activism and movement building (see chapter 10). Do the brief Racial Healing Practice below to explore these roles in your life.

RACIAL HEALING PRACTICE
Moving from "Ally" to "Accomplice" or "Co-Conspirator"

How might you see your activism moving from "ally" status to "accomplice" or "co-conspirator" status? Take a moment to write about that below:

_____

_____

_____

_____

_____

_____

_____

_____

I personally like the words "accomplice" and "co-conspirator"—and they fit where I am with my activism now fighting against racial injustice. As you end this chapter, reflect on these words as you consider the type of freedom fighter that you are now, as well as the type you may want to grow into in the future. Regardless of the terms used, the main point is to continuously learn and strengthen your racial allyship over your life.

RACIAL HEALING WRAP-UP

In this chapter, you learned about allyship and identified what it means to be an antiracist in an ongoing and proactive manner. You reflected on your past experiences of being a racial ally, envisioned future opportunities to be a more effective racial ally, and also had a chance to consider the term "ally" itself and whether there is another word, like "accomplice" or "co-conspirator," that fits you better. In the next chapter, you will build on this healing strategy by seeking out collective racial healing.

CHAPTER 10

Engage in Collective Racial Healing

I live in Atlanta now and I've done racial justice work in the South for the majority of my life, so many of my superheroes for justice are folks who did grassroots organizing in the Southeast, such as Dr. Martin Luther King, Jr. One of his lesser-known quotes is one that guides this last chapter and the racial healing strategy of collective healing:

> *I refuse to accept the view that [hu]mankind is so tragically bound to the starless midnight of racism and war that the bright daybreak of peace and brotherhood [and sisterhood] can never become a reality...I believe that unarmed truth and unconditional love will have the final word.* (Jones 2011, para 17)

With this quote, Dr. King reminds us that for as much as racism feels permanent and never ending, there is hope, peace, and a calling for collective healing from racism that can also be permanent and never ending. This collective healing requires an ongoing commitment to knowing and living the truth of one's racialized experiences of privilege and oppression. This also entails an ongoing practice of love, care, and advocacy as we work with other racial justice allies to develop a more just world based on that "unarmed truth and unconditional love." In previous chapters, you have engaged in racial healing strategies—as a person of color or White person—designed to learn and name the harm that racism has on you, your relationships, and your communities. This chapter builds upon the individual consciousness-raising work you've done (chapter 5) and extends the racial ally strategies you've been building (chapter 9) to help you develop a racial justice community where you can continue to raise your consciousness and promote your healing with a collective of folks who are doing similar work.

WHAT IS A COMMUNITY?

"Community" is a pretty broad term, but generally refers to a group of folks who have commonalities of interests, goals, and perspectives on the world. The main criteria for community is that there is a shared sense of support and fellowship. So, when you think about your communities, who you include as members likely involves a closer examination of your family and friends as well as of work and school relationships.

I like to think of community as my efforts to build a family of choice—people I know who have my back in good times and in challenging times. Communities of choice can be built around the wide variety of social identities you have that we explored in chapter 9. For instance, as a queer person, I have a "family of choice" of people in the LGBTQ+ community with whom I can receive and provide support around my sexual orientation and gender identity. I also have a more distinct family of choice of LGBTQ+ people of color who "get" the intersections of race, gender, and sexual orientation in a way that my White LGBTQ+ friends do not.

Some people love to develop community in person (oftentimes extroverts), and some prefer to access communities one-on-one online, or not at all (oftentimes introverts). Do the next Racial Healing Practice to explore how you feel in general about community and developing community.

RACIAL HEALING PRACTICE
My Relationship to Community

You can be involved in lots of types of communities, from those that have to do with settings you are in (e.g., school, work, neighborhood), which may or may not be of personal value to you, to those that spring from your social identities—race, religion, gender, and so on. Respond to the following prompts.

List some communities of which you are a part right now.

1. _____

2. _____

3. _____

4. _____

5. _____

6. _____

How did you develop the communities you listed above?

_____

_____

_____

_____

_____

What are the rewards of being in these communities?

_____

_____

_____

_____

_____

What are the challenges of being in these communities?

_____

_____

_____

_____

_____

How does your race play a role in these communities? Are your communities people of color, White folks, or a mixture of races? Do you think about your race when you are in these communities? Why or why not?

_____

_____

_____

_____

_____

What did you notice about your communities and their rewards and challenges? Did you want to develop any of these communities further? Did any of your communities have to do with race or your other identities that are important to you? Are there ways you feel supported in your communities, for your racial identity or some other identity that is salient to you, and are there ways you feel disadvantaged in them?

BUILDING A RACIAL JUSTICE COMMUNITY

A racial justice community is a group of people working together on racial healing and accountability endeavors. Developing and being a part of a racial justice community is key to being able to continue the work you've begun doing by using this workbook. Your community will help sow the seeds for the large-scale political action and social change that facilitates others' healing from racism and the dismantling of racist societal structures. As with any type of community you create, building a racial justice community for yourself is a very personal endeavor.

When doing so, it's important to think about your individual needs and interests as a person of color or a White person in relation to community and the potential contributions you want to make. Lots of things can influence these needs, interests, and contributions. You may have needs for community that are related to each of the racial healing strategies in this book—from where you are in your racial identity development and (re)learning the history of racism to grieving racism and reclaiming your whole self. Take a look at the following examples of needs, interests, and contributions related to earlier chapters in this workbook that might apply to you as a person of color or White person. You'll see how the examples range with regard to accessing in-person and online racial justice community and support:

Know Your Racial Identity (chapter 1)
> Connecting with people who are "waking up" to their race.

Explore Your Internalized Racism (chapter 2)
> Attending a group (support group, counseling group, activist group) that intentionally examines how racism is internalized.

(Re)learn the History of Racism (chapter 3)
> Attending community meetings, lectures, workshops, and other events dedicated to new learnings about the local, national, and international history of race and racism as well as how it operates in the present (e.g., prison incarceration rates, housing laws, employment

opportunities, public policy, access to important resources like education and thriving neighborhoods).

Grieve and Name Racism (chapter 4)

Identifying with intention the people in your life you can speak with about the emotions that come up as you become aware of your own racism or internalized racism.

Raise Your Race-Consciousness (chapter 5)

Developing a group of White folks to explore how to use White privilege more effectively, gathering a people of color to identify ways to further excavate and heal internalized racism, or communing with a group of people from different races to have race-conscious conversations together.

Catch Yourself in the Flow of Racism (chapter 6)

Following a set of Twitter accounts (or making your own) to learn about and share instances of covert and overt racism to increase your ongoing awareness and skills to respond in these situations.

Understand Racism in Relationships (chapter 7)

Connecting with individuals or groups of people in your family, friend, work, or school circles to have intentional conversations about race and racism and how these influence your individual relationships.

Reclaim Your Whole Racial Self (chapter 8)

Following a blogger or someone on YouTube who explores their intersection of identities related to race so you can be inspired by their process and implement new ideas related to how your multiple identities intersect with race and racism in your life.

Be a Racial Ally (chapter 9)

Joining a Facebook group or in-person support group dedicated to racial allyship or co-conspiratorship as a White person or person of color.

Hopefully you were inspired by these examples to think of some racial justice communities you might be able to support right away. You may have important passions and commitments that can guide you in determining what kinds of racial justice communities you want to join or build. If you are really passionate about housing justice because of what your own racial identity group has faced in this regard, you could look for an organization that works to this end. As you explored in chapter 9, some of the folks you meet in these organizations can help you develop your own thoughts and perspectives on allyship and being an accomplice and co-conspirator. At different times in my life, I have joined a variety of community groups to help expand my understanding of key racial justice issues. For example, some friends and I worked on the intersection of racism and child sexual abuse for many years. Lately, I have found specific ways to support the #blacklivesmatter movement, and I continue my commitments to immigration and undocumented rights movements. Some of my closest and longest friendships have developed from these spaces, and these friends are a key part of my racial healing journey—whether we are movement building or simply having coffee.

I encourage you to consider ways you can access racial justice communities *both* online and in person. You may be introverted or not have much time to attend a group, so online can be a good place to check in with community for racial healing and accountability. But sometimes, especially during racial crises and explosive incidents of racism in society (local, regional, national, or international), you may need to connect with folks in person for racial healing and accountability. I personally think having a mix of both online and in-person community involvement is best to keep you on track and reflecting on racism. It does take some energy to do both, but you can think of this energy as an investment not only in yourself, but also in the betterment of the world (no pressure!). Seriously, in the end, think about what is best for you and inspires you to take the next steps on your racial healing journey. Do the next Racial Healing Practice to explore how the earlier racial healing strategies in this workbook can involve community support and accountability.

RACIAL HEALING PRACTICE
Making the Connection to Community with Racial Healing Strategies

Identify some possibilities that exist right now for you to participate in racial justice communities in person and online. Most likely, you will need access to a computer while you do this Racial Healing Practice so you can search around to see what exists in your local community and beyond, as well as both online and in-person options for each racial healing strategy.

Know Your Racial Identity (chapter 1)

In-person options: _____

Online options: _____

Explore Your Internalized Racism (chapter 2)

In-person options: _____

Online options: _____

(Re)learn the History of Racism (chapter 3)

In-person options: _____

Online options: _____

Grieve and Name Racism (chapter 4)

In-person options: _____

Online options: _____

Raise Your Race-Consciousness (chapter 5)

In-person options: _____

Online options: _____

Catch Yourself in the Flow of Racism (chapter 6)

In-person options: _____

Online options: _____

Understand Racism in Relationships (chapter 7)

In-person options: _____

Online options: _____

Reclaim Your Whole Racial Self (chapter 8)

In-person options: _____

Online options: _____

Be a Racial Ally (chapter 9)

In-person options: _____

Online options: _____

Looking back at your list above, what are the top three online and in-person communities you could access right now?

Online	In-Person
1. _____	1. _____
2. _____	2. _____
3. _____	3. _____

How was it to go back to earlier racial healing strategies and connect them to the possibilities of racial justice community building? Did you notice that you had a preference for in-person or online possibilities, or did you like a mix of both? How did you feel to identify possible communities to connect with right away: excited, anxious, or something else? It can be challenging to think about joining an in-person group you've never been to before or participating in an online forum of some type, so consider talking it through with a supportive person in your life—or even better, bring them along!

YOUR ROLE IN RACIAL JUSTICE

Remember from chapter 3 that Ibram X. Kendi (2017b) highlights that racist ideas grow out of discriminatory policies, not the other way around. Kendi (2018) also stated, "Today, only a renewed commitment to antiracist policies can save the endangered American project" (para 19). As you develop the racial healing strategies in this workbook, it's important to get involved with racial justice movements that seek to dismantle racist policies.

Having racial justice communities can also provide opportunities for you as a White person or person of color to participate in movements designed to reduce the impacts of racism and increase racial healing for larger communities of people. George Lakey (2016) talks about distinct roles people can play in social justice change within justice movements:

- *Helper*—provides services and skills designed to help those without privilege have increased decision-making power over their lives and understand the systemic oppressions influencing their lives. A helper might be someone who volunteers at the front desk of an LGBTQ+ center.

- *Advocate*—engages in legal methods of social change (e.g., legislative policy, legal challenges to unjust laws and unjust treatment of individuals and communities), builds coalitions to work toward explicitly stated demands for justice, and assesses how these justice demands come to fruition or get stalled. An advocate might be someone who works at a local law or policy center or think tank seeking to influence and shift racially unjust policies.

- *Organizer*—strategically focuses on long-term demands for justice and uses grassroots strategies, leadership development, consensus building, and coalition building to develop specific routes toward justice. An organizer might be someone working to improve relations between people of color and the police in a specific neighborhood over a long period of time.

- *Rebel*—uses protest and street activism as vehicles for social justice change, uses specific measures of nonviolence to challenge people with power and unjust institutions, and focuses on strategically addressing specific issues and injustices in a public manner with a plan for success. A rebel might be a White person who is willing to say the hard things in a racial justice group that people of color feel they can't say or won't be taken seriously if they do.

As you read through these four roles, it's likely that one or more will excite you and put you in your growth zone when it comes to developing a racial justice community and your own racial healing. And one or more will likely be outside of your growth and comfort zones and lead to your danger zone (which, as you learned about in chapter 9, is less helpful for true growth in your racial healing journey). Do the Racial Healing Practice below to reflect on which role you see yourself fitting the best and which ones you might take up infrequently based on racial situations in your life and racialized events in society.

RACIAL HEALING PRACTICE
Exploring My Role in Racial Justice Change

When you think about participating in a racial justice community related to movement building, which one of the four roles fits you best? Respond to the following prompts to explore this.

Are you more of a helper, advocate, organizer, or rebel? Why is this role a good fit for you?

_____

_____

_____

_____

What specific strengths do you have related to this racial justice role that you could share with a racial justice community? List six of them here.

1. _____

2. _____

3. _____

4. _____

5. _____

6. _____

For the three roles in social justice change that don't fit you as much, write a little bit about why this is. Might assuming one of these roles push you into your comfort or danger zones?

_____

_____

_____

_____

As you wrote about the role that fit you the best and the ones that didn't, did you think of any racial justice movements now in which you would like to get involved? How did it feel to write about the strengths you have related to your racial justice role? Were you motivated to contribute these skills to racial justice movements? The thing I like the best about the four social justice roles as applied to racial justice is that you can see that there are many, many different types of people who can fit these roles and make a positive change in challenging racism and reducing its influence on people in your community.

RUPTURES AND RESILIENCE: DEVELOPING A RACIAL JUSTICE COMMUNITY THAT "WORKS" FOR YOU

As you start deepening your work in racial justice communities, you likely will notice right away that there are many folks from very different backgrounds engaged in the work. You may also notice that people have very different perspectives within racial justice communities on "what works" when working toward racial justice. For instance, some people may feel strongly that people of color must be the primary decision makers. Some communities want to organize within their own racial group, while other communities prioritize people of color and White antiracist leadership. Some racial justice communities strategize for the long term, while others have street activism as a primary focus.

I have been part of a team that organizes queer and trans Black and people of color communities in Atlanta on Martin Luther King day. For many years, we had White leaders on our organizing team. But as the Movement for Black Lives picked up and the murders of Black people by police and other police violence gained more media coverage, a need grew for the team to be composed primarily of Black leaders to craft an organizing vision centered on Black queer and trans lives. White allies and other people of color groups still attended the organization's events and were active supporters. As a mixed race, South Asian person, I had open and honest dialogues about whether I should remain as a leader on the team within this community. Ultimately, I stayed, but my efforts shifted to recruiting Black volunteers for the group and maintaining a focus on the issues that impacted Black queer and trans lives. I see this group growing and thriving over time, and I attribute the success of their racial justice efforts to focusing the scope of their leadership and vision on Black issues that ultimately made them more effective.

As my story illustrates, some of these differences can lead to stronger ideas, goals, and convergence of interests within racial justice communities, while other differences can lead to ruptures, hard feelings, and long-lasting misunderstandings. The White leaders and I in my example above could have gotten our feelings hurt, but we had developed the skill of leaning into racial justice conversations with humility and openness. On the other hand, I have seen bad stuff happen in racial justice movements where ruptures have happened. I have seen groups be taken over by well-meaning White allies or by men of color with no awareness of their male privilege. I don't mean to dampen the excitement you are hopefully feeling about getting involved in racial justice movements, but it's something that can happen pretty frequently and I want you to be prepared.

Why do these ruptures happen? Well, I used to get super upset about these ruptures, and now I see them in a different light. I believe that these ruptures happen *exactly when you are doing racial justice work.* I mean how could they not? Racism is a big, entrenched, and dominant system. Seeing our way out of racism is seldom easy, which can feel brutal because of the devastating consequences for so many people of color. In addition, when you work to end racism, you will inevitably step into racial conflict, which can come with not only lots of discomfort, but also often a high risk of failure. Simply put, Western societies just haven't put into action an alternative to racism. So it can feel like the stakes are pretty high when you are working toward collective racial healing.

One of the things I know from my counseling and psychological background is that when the stakes are high, we tend to react with our "smallest self"—trying to protect ourselves, be "right" (or even perfect), and not look bad. I remember when one of my close friends of color was leading a racial justice movement, and she was struggling with some of the self-identified White antiracists who were actually enacting multiple racial microaggressions within the group. My friend wasn't well equipped to respond to these microaggressions, and people of color began to leave the group. The ripple effects of these ruptures continue in our community today.

I can think of another example where a White colleague had worked diligently for years on being a racial ally, and she was criticized by a person of color for something racist she actually had not done. As the passion for racial justice can run high within communities that work on these issues, at times people attack one another and lose track of the overall racial justice goal. You might want to throw your hands up in the air in these moments and say, "Okay, I'm out of here." (See the importance of knowing your racial identity in these situations in chapter 1.) But it is *so* important for us to find moments of reconciliation, forgiveness, and grace with one another as we work toward racial justice. It's not that I want us to pretend that the conflict isn't there. But I do think we need to develop collective strategies of healing and restitution within a group as much as we can, and learn to avoid the impulse to shame and blame others, instead finding ways to understand one another and work toward a common goal.

With that perspective, I take these ruptures less personally. It's not that I have grown a thick skin; I just am able to step back and reflect on how those ruptures might be *exactly* a symptom of racism that is showing up in my relationships and racial justice communities. I think there is a parallel process: there is racism in the world, so naturally it is going to show up in our relationships (as we talked about in chapter 7). It's not the easiest to stay engaged in collective healing when racial ruptures happen, but with this perspective I am able to engage all of the earlier racial healing strategies in this workbook and strive to live in my growth zone. Some of the ruptures you can learn from and be better for—and others require you to set a boundary of what's okay and not okay with you (this often applies to online ruptures that can happen suddenly and unexpectedly with family and friends). Of course, it is best to find ways in racial justice movements to avoid these ruptures and promote group unity, but the truth is the ruptures—big and small—are going to happen. As you've learned in this workbook, the more you are prepared and practice for the resulting products of racism, the more effective you can be in your own and collective racial healing.

I find collective healing tends to take a sideways turn in racial justice movements when you notice the following happening:

- Lack of consensus-building strategies from leadership.

- Silencing of people through asking people not to share their thoughts or feelings on a topic or not giving them appropriate avenues to do so.

- Shame and blame tactics where both White people and people of color aren't leaning into an authentic dialogue about racism and finding key areas of consensus, but rather using call-out culture to point fingers. (This approach fails to recognize the importance of taking accountability for our roles within racism, which entails an openness and curiosity to get to the heart of a racial disagreement.)

- Disorganization and lack of focus where the racial justice goals and strategies are not clear.

- Some people taking up more of the "talk" time than others or dominating the space without leader intervention.

- Limited racial diversity of leaders at the "top," resulting in limited attention to racial diversity in the group's strategic directions and day-to-day operations, which omits key and important perspectives in decision making (i.e., if people of color aren't top leaders, decision making is a White, and thus limited, endeavor).

- Limited awareness or acknowledgment of multiple and intersecting identities in decision making (e.g., valued leaders of color who influence decision making but are not aware of their own identities of privilege, such as male, straight, or cisgender).

- Lack of a framework for understanding racial privilege and oppression as these may manifest in how the organization conducts meetings, considers directions for action, and implements the initiatives it decides on.

Now, the other side of this coin is that when you have many folks from diverse and varied backgrounds and perspectives in racial justice movements, collective healing and goal achievement can happen super-fast and smoothly—usually because the following ingredients are present:

- Ongoing use of a racial privilege and oppression framework—one that is intersectional and attends to multiple identities of privilege and oppression other than race—which guides meetings, gatherings, and other implementation opportunities.

- Community leaders from a diverse and varied background.

- A focus on consensus-building models that all community members are trained in using.

- A mechanism to help new community members meet established community members so they feel included and vital to the group's racial justice goal.

- Accountability mechanisms to prevent potential ruptures and to manage them when they happen (e.g., conflict mediation, dialogue models).

I could list a lot more, but these are the main ones to look out for. For example, when I was working with a fellow group of South Asians on issues of violence, we used a racial justice framework to guide us as we worked on sensitive issues of immigration, racism, and violence. We worked with uncommon allies, such as a wide variety of religious leaders (e.g., Christian, Hindu, Muslim, Sikh) who rarely worked together, which helped expand our own perspectives about how to design interventions. Because there were a multitude of stakeholders, we designed a common mission and processes for decision making and consensus building that everyone could use. We shared our mission statement, goals, and leadership processes with new members and developed strategies to manage ruptures within our community that were inclusive of a variety of South Asian cultural backgrounds.

RACIAL HEALING WRAP-UP

In this final chapter, you explored collective racial healing and why it matters. You reflected on the type of racial justice communities that would be supportive of the next steps on your racial healing journey. You took some time to consider the role you would play in racial justice and liberation movements, as well as how potential ruptures and repairs in these movements can happen. Coming up next in the conclusion, you'll find two Racial Healing Practices that give you space to dream and envision a racially just world.

Time to Dream—What Does a Racially Just World Look Like?

As we come to the end of this workbook, I hope you are realizing that you are not the same person who picked up this workbook in the first place. As you have practiced one racial healing strategy after the next, you have grown and changed in some pretty profound ways in how you think about and respond to racism in your life, communities, and the world, and take on new roles as a racial ally, accomplice, and co-conspirator in the process. And that process of transformation is so cool when you think about it. The system of racism didn't want you to take it on, but you did it anyway. And that is how everything about racism can truly change, and how we can all begin and continue our racial healing. Check in with yourself in the Racial Healing Practice below to see how you have grown.

RACIAL HEALING PRACTICE
My Racial Healing Journey—Growth and Next Steps

Take a moment to reflect on the ways you are different now from when you started this workbook. What have you learned about yourself and how have you grown?

_____

_____

_____

_____

_____

_____

_____

_____

_____

_____

_____

_____

When you think about your next steps in your racial healing journey, what are the five most immediate next steps for you to take to keep increasing your clarity and vision?

1. _____

2. _____

3. _____

4. _____

5. _____

I hope you feel really motivated and inspired after completing this Racial Healing Practice. I hope you are able to see how much you have grown in your own understanding of race and racism in the world and in your own racial healing. By working through this book, you are not only becoming a better version of yourself as a human being on this planet, but you are also developing a better and more clear vision of what racial justice looks like in everyday action. I hope you feel motivated to share the next steps on your racial healing journey with others, because you will encourage them to do the same.

From this perspective of increased clarity, knowledge, and skill building related to directly dismantling and externalizing racism, it's time for you to dream a little bit—or actually a lot. It's one thing to build your racial healing strategies one at a time; this is so vital to your own healing and the healing of others. It's another thing, and just as important, to envision the racially just world you are working toward with all of your efforts. Do this final Racial Healing Practice to identify your vision.

RACIAL HEALING PRACTICE
What Does a Racially Just World Look Like to Me?

Close your eyes and let yourself envision a racially just world. Dream big, remove any barriers that come up, and write your vision here.

_____

_____

_____

_____

_____

_____

_____

_____

_____

_____

_____

_____

_____

_____

_____

_____

_____

_____

Below, write what you need to keep in mind as you work toward your vision of a racially just world.

_____

_____

_____

_____

_____

_____

_____

_____

_____

_____

_____

_____

_____

_____

_____

_____

_____

_____

_____

_____

Now, obviously I can't read what you have written, but I have a strong feeling I would love what you wrote. Don't let your vision of a racially just world stay on these pages. Take it out for a ride to share with others in your life. Post your vision on your bulletin board or somewhere else so you can see what that world actually could look like—it's your dream, and I encourage you to make that dream into reality right now in your world. What would you change, do differently, or do similarly if you were breathing your dream into life?

When it comes to dreams, we are fortunate that some folks have paved the path ahead. For instance, Dr. King had a powerful dream about racial justice for people of color. Central to his dream was that the beloved community of White people and people of color would find racial harmony and healing together. For sure, his dream is not quite realized yet. There is much, much work still to do.

And at the same time, the calls for change and the number of antiracists working toward this change have escalated in the last fifty or so years based on the efforts of folks who were just like you—people who wanted to make what Representative John Lewis calls "good trouble" when it comes to racial injustice. Those freedom fighters from long ago changed everything about the world we live in now. People of color have accessed education in higher numbers than ever before. The United States elected the first Black president. Social justice movements have powerfully used policy advocacy and social media to highlight racial injustices and work toward liberation—from the "Dreamers" (Latinx people without citizenship documentation) to the Movement for Black Lives to Standing Rock and the Dakota Access Pipeline water protectors. People of color lead intersectional, large-scale movements like #metoo (founded by Tarana Burke) and transgender liberation movements (with leaders like Janet Mock, Laverne Cox, and Geena Rocero) that inspire individual-level changes.

Organizations like the National Queer Asian Pacific Islander Alliance (NQAPIA) and Ibram X. Kendi's Antiracist Research and Policy Center work to change racist educational, housing, health, employment, and policing policies. White racial justice advocates like Tim Wise, Jane Elliott, Frances Kendall, Howard Zinn, and Paul Kivel have all called more attention than ever before to issues of White supremacy, educating a new generation on how to become effective and authentic White antiracists in their everyday lives. These changes didn't come out of nowhere; they happened sometimes one step at a time, and other times in leaps and bounds. So in closing this workbook, I would like to share some quotes to remind you to take up the mantle of your racial justice healing—to keep going, to (rest)ore when you need to, and to continue on your racial healing journey with a spirit of love for yourself and others:

We cannot walk alone. And as we walk, we must make the pledge that we shall march ahead. We cannot turn back.

—Martin Luther King, Jr.

Take care how you place your moccasins upon the Earth, step with care, for the faces of the future generations are looking up from the Earth waiting their turn for life.

—Wilma Mankiller

Acknowledgments

Like any journey of racial healing, this book is also a product of many allies, co-conspirators, and accomplices. Huge thanks to Ryan Buresh at New Harbinger, who advocated for this book and encouraged me each step of the way. It literally wouldn't have happened without you. And to associate editor Vicraj Gill, I offer profound gratitude. I never in my wildest dreams imagined I would have a fellow South Asian who would edit with such care, brilliance, and vision. I also greatly appreciate the fine copyediting skills of Rona Bernstein, who made me feel like she cared about this book as much as I do. Thank you to my dear friends Priyanka Sinha (graphic designer for the Racial Healing Wheel) and Darshana Patel, who have kept me on my dharma path as I have written this book. Deep appreciations to Savitri and Aadil Palkhivala, founders of Purna Yoga, whose teachings have helped me aspire, center, and ground. My deepest appreciations to my partner, Lauren Lukkarila, who inspires me with her brilliance each moment. Thank you to my mom, dad, brother, and extended family in India and the US—may our racial healing journeys continue together.

Writing this workbook was a powerful and therapeutic experience. On most days that I was writing, media of all sorts were filled and overflowing with racist events, from White supremacists marching in Charlottesville and protesting the toppling of Confederate statues to murders of Black and Latinx people by police and racial micro- and macroaggressions promoted by leaders at the highest levels of US government. Many talked about the "unprecedented" nature of this racism, but if you know the history of the United States, then you know racism has been insidious, overt, and cruel since its inception. However, what *did* seem unprecedented was the number of people waking up, taking to the streets, and taking everyday action to challenge racism—and I am grateful to all of these people. I was reminded again and again of Arundhati Roy's (2003, 172) words that serve as a racial justice mantra for me: "Another world is not only possible, she is on her way. On a quiet day, I can hear her breathing."

Afterword

When someone pushes racism into my awareness, I feel guilty (that I could be doing so much more); angry (I don't like to feel like I'm wrong); defensive (I already have two Black friends...I worry more about racism that most whites do - isn't that enough); turned off (I have other priorities in my life - with guilt about that thought): helpless (the problem is so big - what can I do?). I HATE TO FEEL THIS WAY. That is why I minimize race issues and let them fade from my awareness whenever possible. (Winter 1977, 24)

As an Asian mother, how do I console my 6-year-old daughter who wants so much to be White, like all the other children in her class? June came home crying yesterday about kids teasing her over the shape of her eyes and other physical features. I told her she was beautiful, although different from the other kids, but it didn't seem to help. I remember going through the same thing...but I suffered in silence. I don't want June to suffer in silence, but what can I say? How do I tell her there is nothing wrong with being Chinese? (Sue 2015, 115)

These two quotations illustrate the complexity of prejudice and the many hot emotional buttons pushed in White Americans and people of color when issues of race, racism, Whiteness and white privilege come to the surface. These nested or embedded feelings of shame, anger, defensiveness, guilt, and pain represent a line of defense that prevents many Whites from exploring their own values, biases, and prejudices toward culturally diverse groups. People of color who are also socialized into a racist society are additionally burdened by a nation that tells them they are lesser human beings, a message that may lead to internalized racism and a belief that they are inferior.

The Racial Healing Handbook: Practical Activities to Help You Challenge Privilege, Confront Systemic Racism, and Engage in Collective Healing by Dr. Anneliese Singh is a much needed and valuable workbook that allows Whites and people of color to understand themselves as racial/cultural beings. The book was written for both Whites and persons of color who wish to heal and liberate themselves from being victimized by a bigoted and intolerant society. The painful cultural conditioning experienced by everyone is enforced and manifested in (a) interactions with significant others, (b) a racially biased educational system, and (c) inaccurate and stereotyped portrayals of people of color in the mass media. In this workbook, Dr. Singh took us on a journey through a series of activities outlined in step-by-step fashion aimed at having readers develop both a nonracist identity and an antiracist identity as well. Each chapter represented a *spoke* in her *racial healing wheel*, and each contained exercises and activities that comprised their own unique challenges.

Through the powerful chapters in her workbook, readers can now better understand themselves as racial/cultural beings, overcome or deal with power and privilege, develop new racially liberated identities, and ultimately become allies in the struggle for equal rights. Although the journey to liberation and healing is an admirable goal, the steps needed to be taken are not easy ones. Many White Americans, for example, have difficulty acknowledging race-related issues because they elicit guilt about their privileged status, threaten their self-image as fair, moral, and decent human beings, and more importantly, suggest that their "unawareness" and "silence" allow for the perpetuation of inequities and harm to people of color. As Sara Winter (1977) suggests, it is simply easier to let such topics fade from consciousness, to not listen or hear the voices of the oppressed, to enter into a "conspiracy of silence," and/or to dismiss, negate, and minimize the experiential reality of people of color. Acknowledging the existence of bigotry, bias, prejudice, and discrimination and hearing the voices of socially devalued groups in our society is the first step in a long journey to healing.

Likewise, it is important for people of color not only to deal with internalized racism, but to realize they are not immune from inheriting racial biases and prejudices. People of color also receive negative racial messages about one another from the larger society that often threaten interracial/interethnic relations and unity. These biases are often played out among different groups of color and may give rise to the "who's more oppressed" trap. Because all oppression is damaging and serves to separate rather than unify, playing the "I'm more oppressed" game is destructive to group unity and counterproductive to combating racism. Further, going through *The Racial Healing Handbook* will allow people of color to realize that White people can be valuable partners in the struggle for equal rights. People of color need to acknowledge and appreciate the fact that many White Americans are eager to help and represent powerful allies. As someone once said, "The enemy is not White Americans, but rather *White supremacy.*"

I congratulate Dr. Singh for creating such an insightful and valuable racism-healing tool kit in which all of us can take to the path to liberation and enlightenment. Going through the workbook has the potential to change the lives of readers; innocence, ignorance, and naiveté will no longer be an excuse to avoid and ignore our responsibility in the journey toward racial healing. While the process of overcoming our racism may occasionally be unpleasant, the potential benefits are many. Those who have undertaken similar journeys often remark that they have personally benefited. They have experienced a broadening of their horizons; increased their appreciation of people (all colors and cultures); become less afraid and intimidated by differences; been able to communicate more openly and clearly with their family, friends, and coworkers; experienced a greater spiritual connectedness with all groups; and become devoted to ending prejudice and discrimination.

There is an old Chinese proverb that states, "A journey of a thousand miles begins but with a single step." As a reader, you have already taken the first step by reading and working through this book.

—Derald Wing Sue, PhD
Professor, Columbia University, and author of
Microaggressions in Everyday Life
New York, NY

References

Alexander, M. 2012. *The New Jim Crow: Mass Incarceration in the Age of Colorblindness.* New York: The New Press.

Atkinson, D. R., G. Morten, and D. W. Sue, eds. 1998. *Counseling American Minorities* (5th ed.) New York: McGraw-Hill.

Baldwin, J. 1955. *Notes from a Native Son.* Boston, MA: Beacon Press.

Banerjee, R., J. G. Reitz, and P. Oreopoulos. 2017. *Do Large Employers Treat Racial Minorities More Fairly? A New Analysis of Canadian Field Experiment Data.* Retrieved from http://www.hireimmigrants .ca/wp-content/uploads/Final-Report-Which-employers-discriminate-Banerjee-Reitz-Oreopoulos -January-25-2017.pdf

Bowleg, L. 2008. "When Black + Lesbian + Woman ≠ Black Lesbian Woman: The Methodological Challenges of Qualitative and Quantitative Intersectionality Research." *Sex Roles* 59: 312–325.

Brown, N. 2017. "115th Congress: House, Senate Leaders, and Demographics." *AM New York*, January 3. Retrieved from https://www.amny.com/news/politics/115th-congress-house-senate-leaders-and-demo graphics -1.12841856

Burmila, E. 2017. "The Invention of Christopher Columbus, American Hero: How the Founding Fathers Turned Christopher Columbus, a Mediocre Italian Sailor and Mass Murderer, into a Historical Icon." *The Nation*, October 9. Retrieved from https://www.thenation.com/article/the-invention-of-christopher -columbus-american-hero/

Campbell, J. 1988. *The Power of Myth.* New York: First Anchor Books.

Cohen, D. 2011. *Braceros: Migrant Citizens and Transnationnal Subjects in the Postwar United States and Mexico.* Chapel Hill, NC: University of North Carolina Press.

Cordoso, J. B. 2010. "Common Themes of Resilience Among Latino Immigrant Families: A Systematic Review of the Literature." *Families in Society* 91 (3): 257–265. doi: http://dx.doi.org/10.1606/1044-3894.4003

Churchill, W. 2002. *Struggle for the Land: Native North American Resistance to Genocide, Ecocide, and Colonization.* San Francisco, CA: City Lights Publishers.

Crenshaw, K. 1989. "Demarginalizing the Intersection of Race and Sex: A Black Feminist Critique of Antidiscrimiantion Doctrine, Feminist Theory and Antiracist Politics." *University of Chicago Legal Forum* 1 (8): 139–167.

Cross, W. E. Jr. 1991. *Shades of Black: Diversity in African-American Identity.* Philadelphia, PA: Temple University Press.

Danticat, E. 2017, May 12. "A Harrowing Turning Point for Haitian Immigrants." *The New Yorker*. Retrieved from https://www.newyorker.com/news/news-desk/a-harrowing-turning-point-for-haitian-immigrants

Georgia Safe Schools Coalition. 2009. *Effective Messaging: Communicating with Parents and School Personnel*. Retrieved from http://www.georgiasafeschoolscoalition.org/images/gssc_manual/effective_messaging _gssc_manual.pdf

Harro, R. 1996. The Cycle of Socialization. In *Diversity and Oppression: Conceptual Frameworks*, edited by M. Adams, P. Brigham, P. Dalpes, and L. Marchesani. Dubuque, IA: Kendall/Hunt.

Helms, J. E. 1990. *Black and White Racial Identity: Theory, Research, and Practice*. New York: Greenwood Press.

Hill-Collins, P. 1990. *Black Feminist Thought*. New York: Routledge.

Hodson, G., J. F. Dovidio, and S. L. Gaertner. 2002. "Processes in Racial Discrimination: Differential Weighting of Conflicting Information." *Personality and Social Psychology Bulletin* 28: 460–471.

Hoffman, J., and J. Hoffman. 2004. "Learning Racial Identity Development Using Human Sculpture." Sculpting Race handout. Long Beach, CA.

hooks, b. 1989. *Talking Back: Thinking Feminist, Thinking Black*. Boston, MA: South End Press.

Jaina, N., L. Orihel, and T. Ross. 2016. *Lessons from Fighting the Black Snake at Standing Rock*. Beulah, CO: Middle Creek Publishing & Audio.

James, M. 2016, January 13. "Are You Racist? 'No' Isn't a Good Enough Answer," YouTube video, 2:15. Retrieved from https://www.youtube.com/watch?v=jm5DWa2bpbs

Jones, C. B. 2011, October 25. "In Tribute to Martin Luther King, Jr: The Opening of the King Memorial," *Huffington Post*. Retrieved from https://www.huffingtonpost.com/clarence-b-jones/martin-luther-king -memorial_b_935060.html.

Kang, S. K., K. A. DeCelles, A. Tilcsik, and S. Jun. 2016. "Whitened résumés: Race and Self-Presentation in the Labor Market." *Administrative Science Quarterly* 61 (3): 1–34. doi: 10.1177/0001839216639577

Kendall, F. E. 2013. *Understanding White Privilege: Creating Pathways to Authentic Relationships Across Race* (2nd ed.). New York: Taylor & Francis.

Kendi, I. X. 2017a. *Stamped from the Beginning: The Definitive History of Racist Ideas in America*. New York: Nation Books.

Kendi, I. X. 2017b, February 5. "Uncovering the Roots of Racist Ideas in America." *The Conversation*. Retrieved from https://theconversation.com/uncovering-the-roots-of-racist-ideas-in-america-71467

Kendi, I. X. 2018. "A House Still Divided." *The Atlantic*, October 2018. Retrieved from https://www.theatlantic .com/magazine/archive/2018/10/a-house-still-divided/568348/

Kivel, P. 2011. *Uprooting Racism: How White People Can Work for Racial Justice* (4th ed.). Gabriola Island, Canada: New Society Publishers.

Kübler-Ross, E., and D. Kessler 2014. *On Grief and Grieving: Finding the Meaning of Grief through the Five Stages of Loss*. New York: Scribner.

Kuramitsu, K. C. 1995. "Internment and Identity in Japanese American Art." *American Quarterly* 47 (4): 619–658. Retrieved from https://www.jstor.org/stable/2713369?seq=1#page_scan_tab_contents

Lakey, G. 2016. "The Four Roles of Relating to Change." *Transformation: Where Love Meets Social Justice*, March 9. Retrieved from https://www.opendemocracy.net/transformation/george-lakey/what-role-were -you-born-to-play-in-social-change

Leavitt, P. A., Covarrubias, R., Perez, Y. A., and Fryberg, S. A. 2015. "Frozen in Time: The Impact of Native American Media Representations on Identity and Self-Understanding." *Journal of Social Issues* 71, 39–53. doi:10.1111/josi.1209

Lee, E. 2016. *The Making of Asian America: A History*. New York: Simon & Shuster.

Little, B. 2018, March 29. "The Most Controversial Census Changes in American History." *History*, March 29, 2018.. Retrieved from https://www.history.com/news/census-changes-controversy-citizenship

Maze, R. L. 2016. *The Invisible Workers of the U.S.–Mexico Bracero Program: Obreros Olvidados*. Lanham, MD: Rowan & Littlefield.

McGrail, K., and M. Rowe Gorosh. 2018. "Cultural Humility: Habit of Mind and Way of Being." Academy of Communication in Healthcare Winter Course on Racism and Equity in Healthcare: Surveying the Landscape and Mapping the Way Forward. Navasota, TX.

Moses, Y. 2017. "Why Do We Keep Using the Word 'Caucasian'"? *Sapiens*, February 1. Retrieved from https://www.sapiens.org/column/race/caucasian-terminology-origin/

NAACP. n.d.. "Criminal Justice Fact Sheet: Racial Disparities in Incarceration." Retrieved from https://www.naacp.org/criminal-justice-fact-sheet/

Neville, H., and W. Cross. 2017. "Racial Awakening: Epiphanies and Encounters in Black Racial Identity." *Cultural Diversity and Ethnic Minority Psychology* 23: 102–108. doi: 10.1037/cdp0000105

Okun, T. 2006. "White Supremacy Culture: Changework." In *Dismantling Racism Workbook*. Retrieved from http://www.cwsworkshop.org/pdfs/CARC/Overview/3_White_Sup_Culture.PDF

Osanloo, A. F., C. Boske, and W. S. Newcomb. 2016. "Deconstructing Macroaggressions, Microaggressions, and Structural Racism in Education: Developing a Conceptual Model for the Intersection of Social Justice Practice and Intercultural Education." *International Journal of Organizational Theory and Development* 4 (1): 1–18.

Phinney, J. S. 1990. "Ethnic Identity in Adolescents and Adults: Review of Research." *Psychological Bulletin* 108: 499–514.

Pierce, C. M. 1970. "Offensive Mechanisms." In *The Black Seventies*, edited by F. Barbour. Boston, MA: Porter Sargent.

Prasad, V. 2001. *The Karma of Brown Folk*. Minneapolis: University of Minnesota Press.

Reeves, R. 2016. *Infamy: The Shocking Story of the Japanese American Internment in World War II*. New York: Picador.

Roediger, D. 2005. *Working Toward Whiteness: The Strange Journey from Ellis Island to the Suburbs*. New York: Basic Books.

Roy, A. 2003. *War Talk*. Cambridge, MA: South End Press.

Sablich, L. 2016. "7 Findings That Illustrate Racial Disparities in Education." *Brookings*, June 6. Retrieved from https://www.brookings.edu/blog/brown-center-chalkboard/2016/06/06/7-findings-that-illustrate -racial-disparities-in-education/

Smith, C. 2018. Twitter post, http://twitter.com/clintsmithIII, May 18, 3:19 p.m.

Stanford Center on Poverty and Inequality. 2018. *State of the Union: The Poverty and Inequality Report.* Retrieved from https://inequality.stanford.edu/sites/default/files/Pathways_SOTU_2018.pdf

Sue, D. W. 2010. *Microaggressions in Everyday Life: Race, Gender, and Sexual Orientation.* New York: Wiley.

Sue, D. W. 2015. *Race Talk and the Conspiracy of Silence: Understanding and Facilitating Difficult Dialogues on Race.* Hoboken, NJ: John Wiley & Sons.

Sue, D. W., C. M. Capodilupo, G. C. Torino, J. M. Bucceri, A. M. B. Holder, K. L. Nadal, and M. Esquilin. 2007. "Racial Microaggressions in Everyday Life: Implications for Clinical Practice." *American Psychologist* 62 (4): 271–286. doi: 10.1037/0003-066X.62.4.271

Tran, A. G. T. T., and R. M. Lee. 2015. "You speak English Well! Asian Americans' Reactions to an Exceptionalizing Stereotype." *Journal of Counseling Psychology* 61 (3): 484–490. doi: http://dx.doi.org/10.1037/cou0000034

U.S. Department of Justice. 2016. "Hate Crime Statistics." Retrieved from https://ucr.fbi.gov/hate-crime/2016/topic-pages/incidentsandoffenses

Vox, L. 2018. "3 Major Ways Slaves Showed Resistance to Slavery." *ThoughtCo,* September 7. Retrieved from https://www.thoughtco.com/ways-slaves-showed-resistance-to-slavery-45401

Walker, V. S. 2018. *The Lost Education of Horace Tate: Uncovering the Hidden Heroes Who Fought for Justice in Schools.* New York: The New Press.

Wazni, A., and A. Beckmann. 2015. "Muslim Women in America and Hijab: A Study of Empowerment, Feminist Identity, and Body Image." *Social Work* 60 (4): 325–333. doi: https://doi.org/10.1093/sw/swv033

Welteroth, E. (Ed.) 2017, May. "Chance the Rapper Opens Up About What It's Like to Challenge Kanye West." *Teen Vogue.* Retrieved from https://www.teenvogue.com/story/chance-the-rapper-jordan-peele-cover-interview-music-issue-creativity.

Widner, S., and S. Chicoine. 2011. "It's All in the Name: Employment Discrimination Against Arab Americans." *Sociological Forum* 26 (4): 806–823. doi: http://dx.doi.org.proxy-remote.galib.uga.edu/10.1111/j.1573-7861.2011.01285.x

Winter, S. 1977. "Rooting Out Racism." *Issues in Radical Therapy* 17: 24–30.

Wise, T. 2011. *White Like Me: Reflections on Race from a Privileged Son.* Oakland, CA: Soft Skull Press.

Wise, T. 2012. *Dear White America: Letter to a New Minority.* San Francisco, CA: City Lights Publishers.

Wolf, S. 2018, November 29. "Daily Kos Elections Presents Our Comprehensive Guide to the 116th Congress Members and Districts." Retrieved from https://www.dailykos.com/stories/2018/11/29/1815960/-Daily-Kos-Elections-presents-our-comprehensive-guide-to-the-116th-Congress-members-and-districts

Zinn, H. 2005. *A People's History of the United States.* New York: HarperCollins.

Anneliese A. Singh, PhD, LPC, is a professor and associate dean of diversity, equity, and inclusion in the college of education at the University of Georgia. Singh is cofounder of the Georgia Safe Schools Coalition to work on reducing heterosexism, transprejudice, racism, and other oppressions in Georgia schools. She founded the Trans Resilience Project, where she translated her findings from nearly twenty years of research on trans people's resilience to oppression into practice and advocacy efforts. She is author of *The Queer and Transgender Resilience Workbook*. She's delivered widely viewed TEDx Talks, and recorded a podcast for the American Psychological Association on her research with transgender youth and resilience.

Foreword writer **Tim Wise** is among the nation's most prominent antiracist essayists and educators. He has spent the past twenty-five years speaking to audiences in all fifty US states, at more than 1000 college and high school campuses, at hundreds of professional and academic conferences, and to community groups across the nation. He has lectured internationally in Canada and Bermuda, and has trained corporate, government, law enforcement, and medical industry professionals on methods for dismantling racism in their institutions.

Afterword writer **Derald Wing Sue, PhD**, is professor of psychology and education in the department of counseling and clinical psychology at Teachers College and the School of Social Work, Columbia University. He is a pioneer in the field of multicultural psychology, multicultural education, multicultural counseling and therapy, and the psychology of racism/antiracism.

Real change *is* possible

For more than forty-five years, New Harbinger has published proven-effective self-help books and pioneering workbooks to help readers of all ages and backgrounds improve mental health and well-being, and achieve lasting personal growth. In addition, our spirituality books offer profound guidance for deepening awareness and cultivating healing, self-discovery, and fulfillment.

Founded by psychologist Matthew McKay and Patrick Fanning, New Harbinger is proud to be an independent, employee-owned company. Our books reflect our core values of integrity, innovation, commitment, sustainability, compassion, and trust. Written by leaders in the field and recommended by therapists worldwide, New Harbinger books are practical, accessible, and provide real tools for real change.

newharbingerpublications

MORE BOOKS *from*
NEW HARBINGER PUBLICATIONS

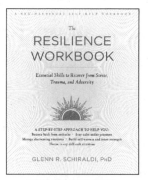

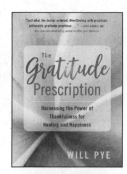

Register your **new harbinger** titles for additional benefits!

When you register your **new harbinger** title—purchased in any format, from any source—you get access to benefits like the following:

- Downloadable accessories like printable worksheets and extra content

- Instructional videos and audio files

- Information about updates, corrections, and new editions

Not every title has accessories, but we're adding new material all the time.

Access free accessories in 3 easy steps:

1. Sign in at NewHarbinger.com (or **register** to create an account).

2. Click on **register a book**. Search for your title and click the **register** button when it appears.

3. Click on the **book cover or title** to go to its details page. Click on **accessories** to view and access files.

That's all there is to it!

If you need help, visit:

NewHarbinger.com/accessories

new harbinger
CELEBRATING
40 YEARS